The Telegraph

all new CRYPTIC CROSSWORDS

An Hachette UK Company
www.hachette.co.uk

First published in Great Britain in 2012 by
Hamlyn, a division of Octopus Publishing Group Ltd
Endeavour House, 189 Shaftesbury Avenue
London WC2H 8JY
www.octopusbooks.co.uk

ISBN 978-0-600-62500-1

A CIP catalogue record for this book is available from the British Library.

Printed and bound by CPI Group (UK) Ltd, Croydon, CR0 4YY

10 9 8 7 6 5 4 3 2

Acknowledgements
Telegraph Puzzle Editor: Philip McNeill
Editorial Director: Trevor Davies
Senior Editor: Joanne Wilson
Designer: Eoghan O'Brien
Editorial Assistant: Pauline Bache
Page make up: Dorchester Typesetting Group Ltd
Production: Peter Hunt, Davide Pontiroli

The Telegraph 2

all new CRYPTIC CROSSWORDS

A new collection of **100** entertaining, stimulating and challenging puzzles

hamlyn

Editor's note

Welcome to the latest *Telegraph Cryptic Crosswords* book. I hope you'll enjoy the 100 puzzles inside.

I've had the privilege of editing the *Telegraph* Crossword for three years, and it's nice to have the opportunity to pay tribute to the compilers who have made it an institution.

The *Telegraph*'s best-known setter is Roger Squires, the world's most prolific compiler. A former Fleet Air Arm lieutenant, professional magician and television actor, Roger has written two million clues and compiled 1,000 *Telegraph* Crosswords.

Then we have Don Manley, the author of the *Chambers Crossword Manual*; Peter Chamberlain, who recently celebrated 25 years as the *Telegraph*'s Saturday setter; and Jeremy Mutch, who compiled his 500th *Telegraph* crossword last year. Between them those four have clocked up 70 years with the *Telegraph*, and you'll find dozens of their puzzles in this book.

Apart from cartoonists, no one in newspapers gives readers so much pleasure – if 'pleasure' is the right word for the mental torture of crossword-solving. We hope you'll be teased, entertained and pleasantly tortured by the puzzles in this book.

Happy solving from all on the *Telegraph* crossword team.

Phil McNeill
Telegraph Crossword Editor

Puzzles

Across

1 Boasting about new halo, ultimate reason for praise (8,5)
10 Bird heading North to a city in Italy (7)
11 Housing monarch in a little row of houses (7)
12, 13 & 14 Author's crazy animal trapped between cars (4,5,4)
13 See 12
14 See 12
17 I.e. to go over time after time after time (7)
18 Gets off the road and rests for the night (5,2)
19 Telling jokes without lying? (5-2)
22 Part of this event happens after six (7)
24, 25 & 26 Virtuous royal female getting chap away from chaperone? (4,5,4)
25 See 24
26 See 24
29 Fashionable mission in US, extremely delicate (1,2,4)
30 Head off from part of Russia or Africa? Actually, from part of Western Europe (7)
31 Call for help as lad at home runs amok (5,3,5)

Down

2 Religious education with part of Bible? Just the opposite! (7)
3, 15 & 27 Totally triumphs as one among bridge players with cards on the table? (4,5,4)
4 My declaration of friendship in Arab country (7)
5 Become disorientated and beat it! (3,4)
6, 16 & 28 Disastrous poll is very 'ard for senior politician (4,5,4)
7 Grounds are ruined by boys (7)
8 Fast car I fling about, showing control on the road (7,6)
9 Leader bunkered, unable to see the problem? (4,2;3,4)

1

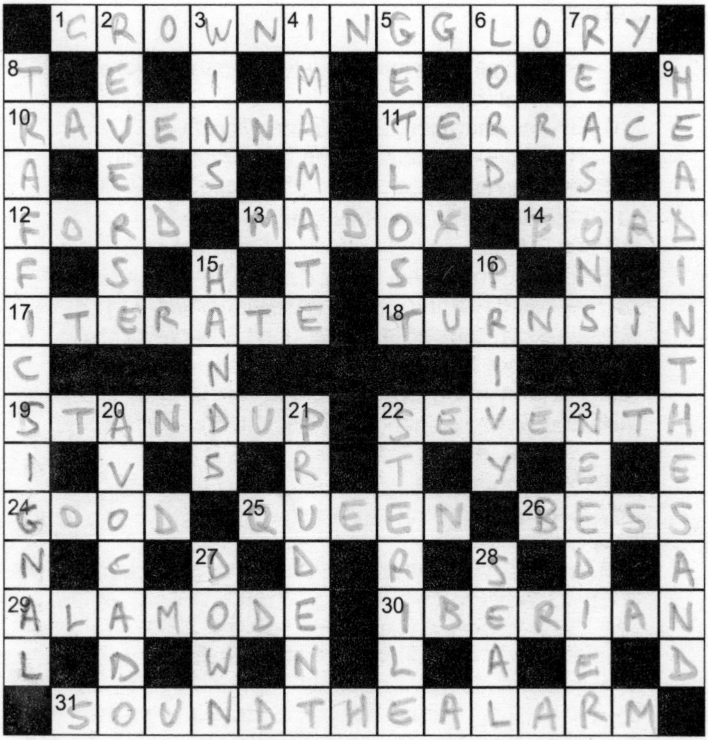

15 See 3
16 See 6
20 Fruit producing 'orrible mess and bother (7)
21 Puritan with sacred books, wise and cautious (7)
22 Lacking inspiration, as theatre usually is (7)
23 Less prosperous poet's never accepting decline (7)
27 See 3
28 See 6

Across

4 Achieve personal advancement through good work with student experts (2,6)
8 A metal container found in father's coat (6)
9 Listen to indeterminate ramblings from people who wander (8)
10 Requirement to steal identity? (8)
11 Catch some coming back after opponents (6)
12 Wave around cereal bowl? (8)
13 The likely cost if it is French individual to marry (8)
16 Reverse target, accepting a long tricky colour (8)
19 Oils, oddly, found in lots of treacle (8)
21 Good ruling welcoming everybody from France! (6)
23 Exterior wall painting by a student (8)
24 Boundary dispute? (8)
25 Show home initially chosen taken by nightfall (6)
26 Constant part of garden tableware (8)

Down

1 Food that's a manifestation of avarice? (7)
2 Understanding evil, ruler has pain cut by half (7,2)
3 Footballers wearing Indian dress for big game trip! (6)
4 Reveal a secret present and the match is off (4,3,4,4)
5 Colours in springtime perhaps lacking reds and indigos initially (8)
6 Stop a container loading sulphur (5)
7 Pull out of additional court case (7)
14 Public communications service raised help to protect the compiler (4,5)
15 The menu's in French! (1,2,5)
17 Unpaid, you are rumoured to support a friend (7)
18 Baltic rooster and fish (7)
20 Elated at being arrested! (6)
22 The science of one involved in clog dancing (5)

2

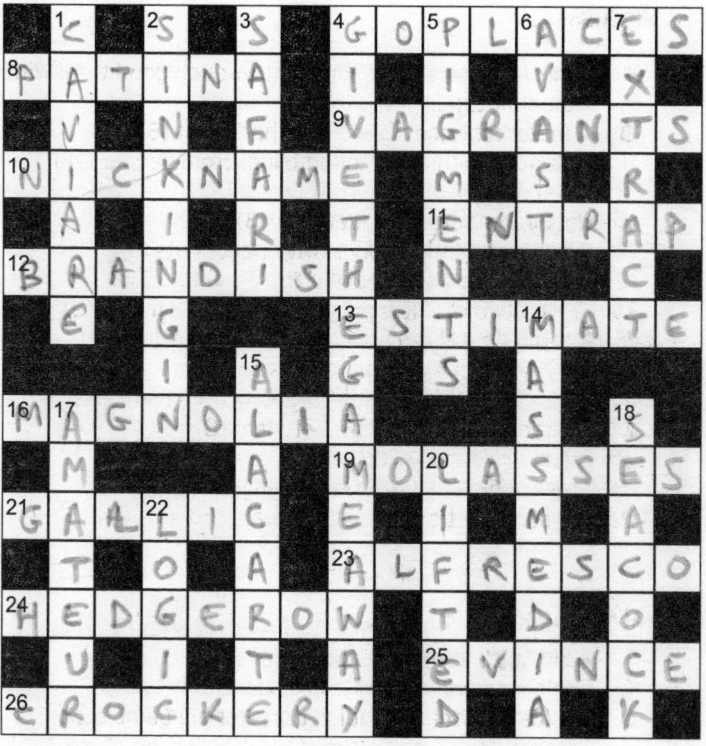

Across

1 Stand on the breakfast table (5,4)
9 Lady collecting silver - what's amount spent? (6)
10 Label for the ham maybe? (5,4)
11 Disease making naval captain tense (6)
12 View admissions of debt as flippant (9)
13 Sheep on motorway - into it goes one woman (6)
17 Go very quietly round end of lane (3)
19 Peter's nine mates stupidly getting drunk? (15)
20 Funny guy with little sex appeal (3)
21 Man sitting in tree - position for a lord (6)
25 Hardy Adam undone by snake (9)
26 Bathroom - note something useful there (6)
27 Confused in Irish fens, they complete the course (9)
28 Full of passion a brief time, then 'orrendous (6)
29 Overwhelmingly powerful places in Ireland (5-4)

Down

2 Criminal's expenditure almost entirely on wife (6)
3 Writer who makes his mark (6)
4 Gambling centre attracting Irish painter (6)
5 A motion picture's transformed on account of digital processing (15)
6 As a bossy official, I get a rule re-enacted (9)
7 Came to a deal with pub and profited (9)
8 A stiff-faced cast (5,4)
14 Fifty-one, with competence, becoming a nuisance! (9)
15 Sensational people running the company? Right! (9)
16 Help to get Mad Monica inside compound (5,4)
17 Seat that's amazing - not hard! (3)
18 Light touch from boy or girl (3)
22 Murderer, a male turning raving mad (6)
23 Cunning journalist, not straight (6)
24 Distant line of houses generating litter (6)

3

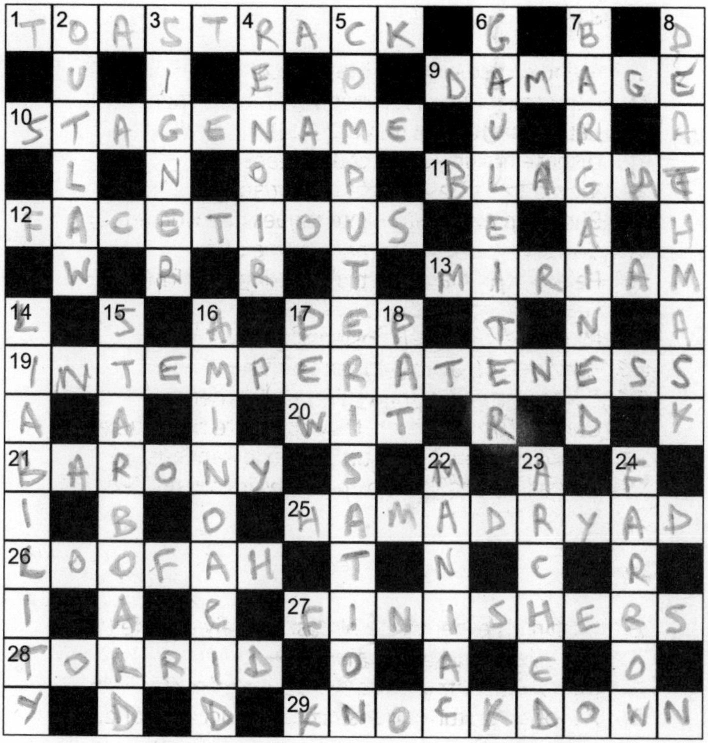

Across

1 Service stalls appealing to large number of people (4-6)
6 Preserve black sidepiece (4)
9 Resinous substance reportedly hits roof first (7-3)
10 Departing losing single medal (4)
12 Opener major receives (3,2,3,4)
15 Score went in the Oriental heard (6)
16 Put on record (8)
18 Warmer in the house perhaps (8)
19 So grieves audibly at the trial (6)
21 Not a good-looking one to serve (4,8)
24 Small creature found source of water not in Welsh town (4)
25 Can a misfit develop excessive enthusiasm? (10)
26 Pair you brought back of hunted animals (4)
27 Spend time in characteristic manner in corridor (10)

Down

1 Tom's troubled but not in the least (4)
2 Fly upwards in this way on arrival (4)
3 Way into the sea? (4,8)
4 Reginald and I take on district (6)
5 Old lawsuit involving exorbitant demand (8)
7 One regrets being this (10)
8 Dictatorial authority that's relatively large? (3,7)
11 Confiscating band of gold after search in bishop's domain (12)
13 Drunk on horseback (7-3)
14 Go first, have quick look at grey mineral (4-6)
17 Country nawab's to reorganise (8)
20 State gold was found in swampy ground (6)
22 Rival went initially to watch (4)
23 Part of poem mysteriously receives award (4)

4

1 M	A	2 S	S	3 M	A	4 R	K	5 E	T	■	6 J	7 A	M	8 B
O	■	O	■	A	■	E	■	X	■	■	■	P	■	I
9 S	E	A	L	I	N	G	W	A	X	■	10 G	O	N	G
T	■	R	■	N	■	I	■	C	■	11 S	■	L	■	B
■	■	■	12 K	E	Y	O	N	T	H	E	D	O	O	R
13 S	■	14 L	■	N	■	N	■	I	■	Q	■	G	■	O
15 T	W	E	N	T	Y	■	16 D	O	C	U	M	E	N	T
I	■	A	■	R	■	17 B	■	N	■	E	■	T	■	H
18 R	A	D	I	A	T	O	R	■	19 A	S	S	I	Z	E
R	■	G	■	N	■	T	■	20 M	■	T	■	C	■	R
21 U	G	L	Y	C	U	S	T	O	M	E	R	■	■	■
P	■	A	■	E	■	W	■	R	■	R	■	22 V	■	23 E
24 C	O	N	Y	■	25 F	A	N	A	T	I	C	I	S	M
U	■	C	■	■	■	N	■	S	■	N	■	E	■	M
26 P	R	E	Y	■	27 P	A	S	S	A	G	E	W	A	Y

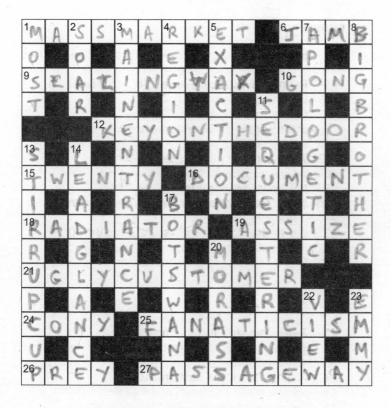

Across

1 Remedial needlework (11)
9 Ex-prime minister happy to put on weight (9)
10 Hopeless – lacking purpose (2,3)
11 Danced and swam (6)
12 The dog one has to register is a boxer (8)
13 Put in charge at the lemonade factory? (6)
15 Flirting, having no head for marriage (8)
18 Vainly seeking masculine attention (8)
19 Master-switch for the current (6)
21 Ships, and in them, pirates (8)
23 It limits the movement of stock (6)
26 A capital position to be in (5)
27 Polite inclination to support royalty (5,4)
28 It assists the diver to go up rather than down (11)

Down

1 Regalia thrown out by republic (7)
2 American needs time for practice (5)
3 Withdraw from the case (9)
4 Short cut taken when hunting (4)
5 Exploit at length, advantageously (8)
6 Boredom in endless night in France (5)
7 Ether may be found around at this place (7)
8 Meeting house (8)
14 Paid back though completely in debt (8)
16 Pregnant member of society? (2,3,4)
17 Director has the staff dressed in purple – royalty coming (8)
18 The standing of a taxi-driver (3-4)
20 Just working tired me (7)
22 A side order for helpers (5)
24 Bertha, if asked, provides port (5)
25 Flat-iron? (4)

5

Across

7 Rest cue bridging centre of black (9)
8 Drain second jug (5)
10 Purity from alcohol, in essence (8)
11 Cabinet seal by Queen (6)
12 Part of old tree contains new pine (4)
13 Model secretary's behind (8)
15 Sort of cut chance in gamble (7)
17 Humble Conservative leader's career (7)
20 Drunk, so easing worries (8)
22 Impulsive right remains... (4)
25 ...group that is offensive... (6)
26 ...with left suffering decline (8)
27 Racist shot in scrap (5)
28 Firmer cane hurts badly (9)

Down

1 Sit up following ace storyteller (5)
2 Gambling club company admits a crime (6)
3 Give line out showing lure (8)
4 God holding new Sunday mass? (7)
5 'Labour' hero? The man governs, round about (8)
6 A number spotted catching match (9)
9 Missile contains large bang (4)
14 Terribly poor signs for doctor's opinion (9)
16 Con isn't troubled receiving a sentence (8)
18 Hear a gun shot for broadside (8)
19 One extremely dead after quarantine (7)
21 Soaks up casserole (4)
23 Root of nerve, say (6)
24 Savings account returning capital (5)

6

REMAINDER
SEWER
HOLINESS
LOCKER
LONG
TEMPLATE
BRISKET
CHASTEN
AGONISES
RASH
SORTIE
LANGUISH
BIGOT
STAUNCHER

Across

1 Knights are members of the Board (8)
9 As ark in fix, firmly boarded the ship (8)
10 A follower on the edge of the verge (4)
11 Lament matter concerning bullying (12)
13 It's unique not to look too closely (8)
15 In Colorado a virtuoso originates an intaglio (6)
16 The two states of seaweed (4)
17 Toast Gordon! (5)
18 Eyes dour abuse regularly (4)
20 Former spouse I directed to be outlawed (6)
21 Birds - spotted fliers (8)
23 A strict Cairo practice belonging to the privileged (12)
26 A French business in Scotland is remarkable (4)
27 Fragment of nothing but a skin layer of cells (8)
28 Occasion to fish before nightfall (8)

Down

2 Plant a malcontent in the House of Lords (8)
3 Gymnastic Samuel strums then leaps about (12)
4 I object to Alan, for instance, finding the maize (6)
5 Not off-side but close (4)
6 Graze caused by adult underwear I put on (8)
7 A keen gardener locates this tree (4)
8 Issues about sedition (8)
12 Computer component with extremely small perimeter (12)
14 Finishes up at the highest place in the ship (5)
16 Means to affirm the time (8)
17 Wrap of eiderdown (8)
19 Poised with a weapon in poor neighbourhood (8)
22 Power unit the French use materially on the roof (6)
24 Idaho and New York lock horns to hold a motor race (4)
25 Frozen dew I'm surrounded by again (4)

7

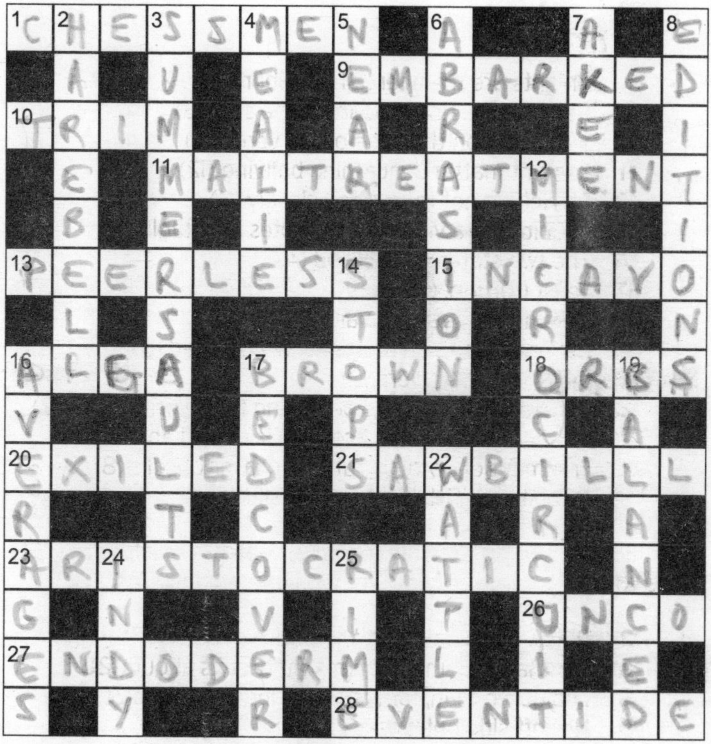

Across

1 Bedroom chats about being out of action (4,2,6)
8 Putting a price on a Liberal university (fashionable) in very good surroundings (7)
9 Leave the coach having been instructed to promote the last two (7)
11 Provincial firm's first class return for capital (7)
12 A dramatic scene - the board get gold! (7)
13 Company at last invested in new look with new fabric (5)
14 Criticise decrease in value without one (9)
16 Rabble-rouser who expected to welcome oriental giant (9)
19 Unhappy hour, oddly, for an ascetic (5)
21 The Vatican perhaps achieved clean break with victory in Europe (7)
23 Finish in Fife, poor but with honourable title (7)
24 View lost, we hear, due to fog (3,4)
25 Inscription from old record - it needs a quiet hour! (7)
26 All upset over badly-knitted jumpers (4-8)

Down

1 Spiral shaped lilac given to ambassador (7)
2 Checks concerned with fashionable crime (5,2)
3 Ruthless boxers welcome feed (3-3-3)
4 Trainee soldier from America detained (5)
5 Lame - but can be changed (7)
6 A weak attorney finds a way through the trees (7)
7 Still at home? Good! Put some clothes on, but what to wear? (7-5)
10 Affluent oriental supporting new French upstart (7,5)
15 Portion the food bit by bit? (9)
17 Refusal to support holy city with this building material (7)
18 Tearing out from hard rock! (7)

8

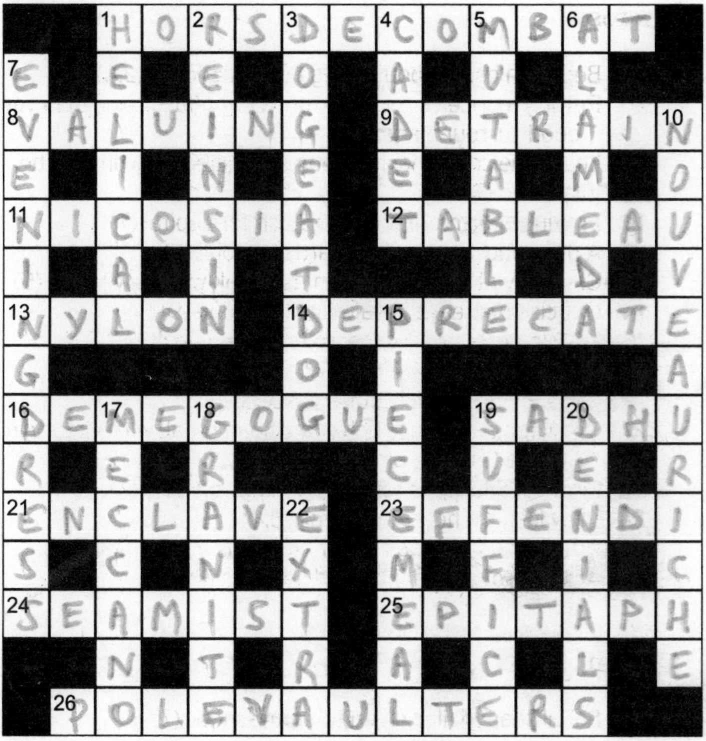

19 Almost be ill, eating one cold – that will be enough (7)
20 Agreements to protect province result in rejections (7)
22 Surplus old paintings put up (5)

Across

1 Expression of resignation by plodder, one quick to know the score (5-6)
7 Sun attracts enthusiastic throng (5)
8 Perplexed and stymied if sent the wrong way (9)
10 Facts about English sailors in hellish situation (7)
11 There's no scoring with these girls (7)
12 Somewhere to swim at far end of the town (5)
13 Sort of earthenware in no store surprisingly (9)
16 A dramatic incident follows mother producing sword (9)
18 Terrorists in Jerusalem – a fiasco (5)
19 Relief money about to be collected in pubs for natives (7)
22 Rifle in one market at the front (7)
23 Temperate part of the globe (9)
24 Stars love performing outside science institution (5)
25 Shows compassion for missy – she apt to break down (11)

Down

1 One could accommodate members of the NUT (9)
2 Sort of plant to have sticker on? (3,4)
3 Play for time, giving office worker zero increase (9)
4 Course dealt with various poems (5)
5 Welshman tells fibs, according to the papers (7)
6 Institute's commendation quietly ignored (5)
7 Problem with spine hit last week? (7,4)
9 Man facing surgery with nothing to lose – hopeless state (11)
14 Defeat finished with one of the strikers in the box (9)
15 Old female darts across motorway, getting out of bounds (3-6)
17 I sat befouled with mud in sports field (7)
18 Vegetables spoil – lines of them in garden (7)
20 Man is buried under lair (5)
21 The female graduate in a wealthy old place (5)

9

Across

1 Spread found on board that cannot be eaten (10)
6 Wrong to have veil twisted (4)
9 Part of service charge, part of service (10)
10 Attorney leaves girl in valley (4)
12 Go arm-in-arm at university union (4-2)
13 Clues to a violent kiss (8)
15 Decide to cooperate and join the queue (4,4,4)
18 Collector's item from the paper? (5,7)
21 Pass position by railway for pit (8)
22 Move quickly on or off (6)
24 Steer over most of one county shortly (4)
25 Expense incurred casually? (10)
26 Lad held ring readily (4)
27 Seclusion at the end of one's career (10)

Down

1 Rugby player's gear (6)
2 If I am quick I shall not – have a rightful place (6)
3 Willpower? (12)
4 Latvian gave permit to Middle Eastern (4)
5 Minute part following 999 (10)
7 Inclined to blow one's top (8)
8 Wildcat I'd reportedly followed having keen sight (4-4)
11 Suddenly and inexplicably appearing from non-existent place (3,2,7)
14 It is not a first time happening (10)
16 Generous father in South Carolina promises to pay (8)
17 Rich spring to be acceptable (4-2-2)
19 Astute misrepresentation of figure (6)
20 Swiss Cottage (6)
23 Small part of the administration (4)

10

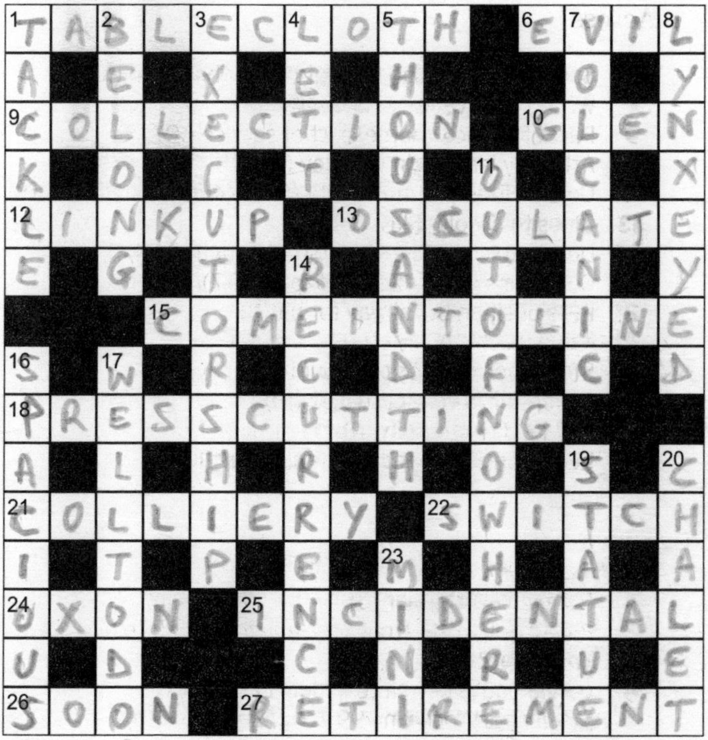

Across

1 Files put in the wrong order with malicious intent (8)
6 A niche for a fellow about fifty (6)
9 Lie, in an open sort of way (6)
10 Number meet for break round northern building (8)
11 Extra decoration on three articles of worsted material (8)
12 Conclude with a feature on charm (6)
13 He cheats - using more than one pack of cards? (6-6)
16 They give light support, though quite powerless (12)
19 Performs a new ascent (6)
21 Official coroner struck down, died (2,6)
23 Compellingly kind (8)
24 One's characteristics begin holding one back (6)
25 Not only on the cricket field will it go to fine leg (6)
26 Insisted order is order (8)

Down

2 Timber producer well-liked but not socially acceptable (6)
3 A capital investment (5)
4 A hand appreciated by a theatre manager (4,5)
5 Drop of leave before autumn (3,4)
6 Her weapon was of no use in a manhunt (5)
7 They're responsible for split sides but firm middles (9)
8 Grape producers include a label to mark their years (8)
13 Taking away Sherlock Holmes' secret of success (9)
14 An extraordinary deed or act may get you this (9)
15 An individual consumer (8)
17 Idea for consideration (7)
18 Soldiers holding deserter without charge (6)
20 Personal column? (5)
22 Length of pitch for batting after tea (5)

11

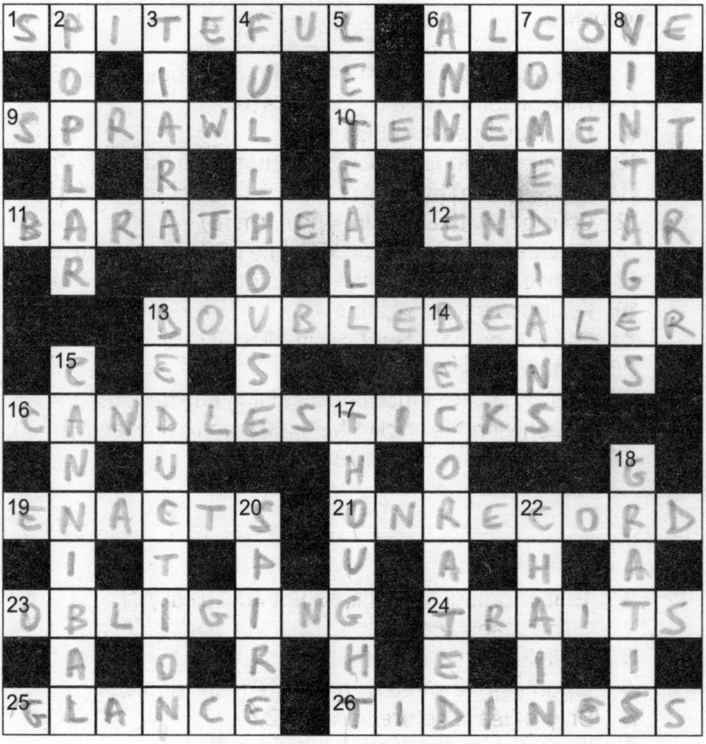
SPITEFUL
ALCOVE
SPRAWL
TENEMENT
BARATHEA
ENDEAR
DOUBLEDEALER
CANDLESTICKS
ENACTS
UNRECORD
OBLIGING
TRAITS
GLANCE
TIDINESS

Across

1 Massive reduction in fossil fuel (8)
5 Headed detective department on rank (6)
9 Melancholy miss back in time (8)
10 Swirl jar holding last of shandy (6)
11 Hearing things? (8)
12 Angry about female despoiled (6)
14 Beat Iran or let loose instability (10)
18 Sit and release terrible winds! (10)
22 Distant country, say (6)
23 Painting left artist with sex appeal (8)
24 Right-leaning type? (6)
25 Serious sport – English taking on Madrid? (8)
26 Fat and gross with prosperity (6)
27 Alcoholic drink catches loyal regular (8)

Down

1 Tries to borrow pounds, accepting penny (6)
2 Attraction including good man's brilliance (6)
3 Left and right initially constrained by state earnings (6)
4 Be out drunk with a limo car (10)
6 Eccentric, I play act bizarrely (8)
7 It's obvious following 'Tea, vicar?' (8)
8 Cringing from Democrat making out (8)
13 Tories' rule potentially doubtful (10)
15 Getting cute? (8)
16 Grounds to accept setter's judgement (8)
17 Recovers with fantastic miracles (8)
19 Capital of Yugoslavia, then Serbia (6)
20 Life line? (6)
21 'Slow and dense', admits Tory leader (6)

12

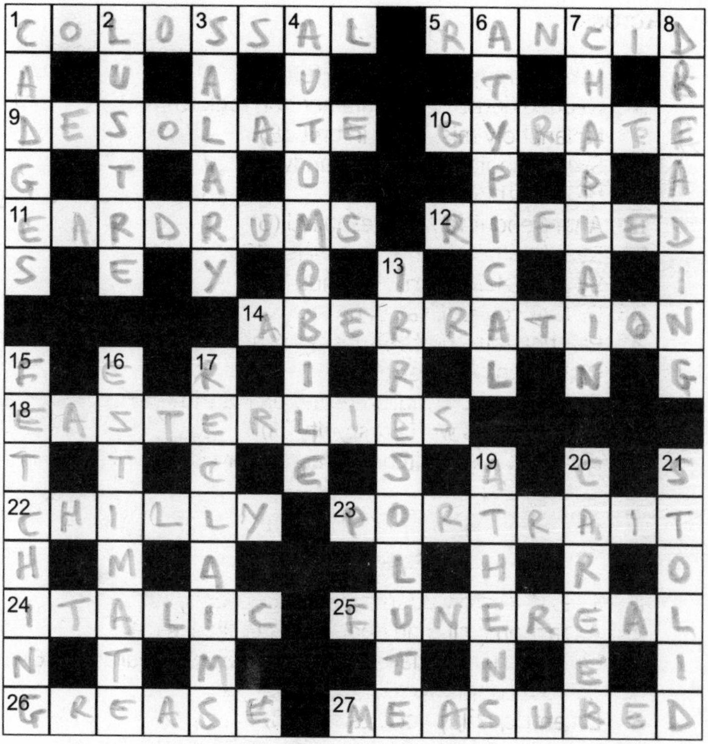

Across

8 Ring the Parisian in boat being loaded (7)
10 Bird, variegated sort one's seen on church (7)
11 Play short tune, hit by Abba initially (9)
12 Confused impression given by book publisher's hype (5)
13 Good man presented with one German beer mug (5)
14 It's featured in West African fetish for unarmed combat (2-5)
17 A remake of timeless Mountie film (4,2,2,2,5)
19 Musical instruction at an end, sadly (7)
21 Child in river having capsized boat (5)
24 Solitary type in cell one, reading (5)
26 Remarkable things – father describes number collected by macho types (9)
27 Rodney, perhaps, might mean very well by dropping out (7)
28 Typical of girl kept in a long time (7)

Down

1 Archbishop Lang's world? (6)
2 Sweet's centre (5-3)
3 Star actor directing soldier (7,3)
4 Sharon and Jo prepared to eat good Indian dish (5,4)
5 Shot in street, a bishop (4)
6 Animosity beginning to tell in card game (6)
7 Left university in ancient city in a depressed state (3,5)
9 Catch some coming over (4)
15 Happy chappie producing a flag (5,5)
16 Fruit that might go off? (9)
17 US singer encountered crossing a lounge (4,4)
18 Relatives, American, in the US itself (5,3)
20 Energetic type wanting Monday off (6)

13

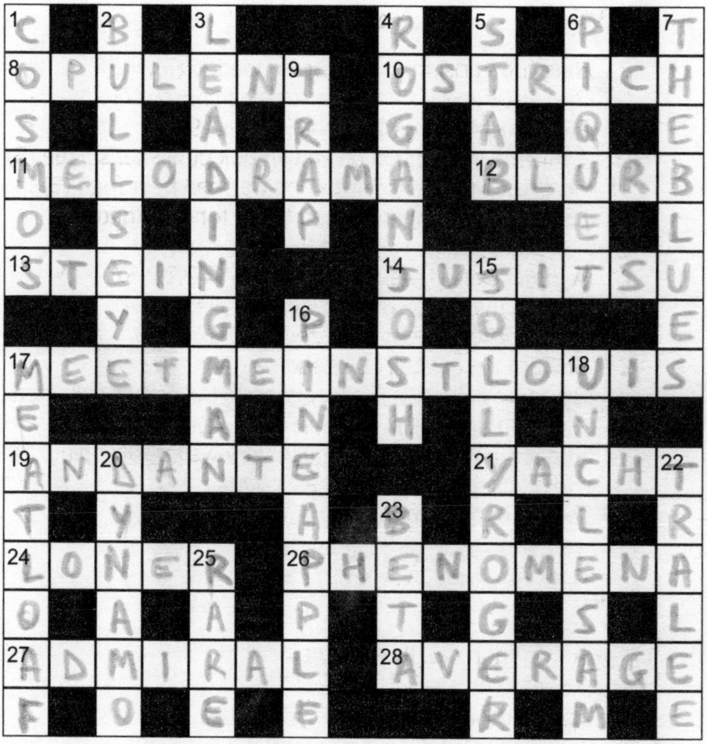

22 An Irish bay – bay, say, skirting a lake (6)
23 Put money on a Greek character (4)
25 Artist, getting on, is seldom seen (4)

Across

1 Royal couple eat perch caught by one of these, perhaps (10)
6 Frank writer on love (4)
10 One makes bundles from the French in drinking establishment (5)
11 Limit the amount of beer with this explanation (9)
12 Put the heat on a tabloid newspaper and get exposure (7)
13 Fighting back, dish out unfair treatment (3,4)
14 People grow old – or it's a change for this relationship! (6,1,5)
18 Alec's beer cue became a notorious incident! (5,7)
21 Even soldiers pull back in front of a river (7)
23 Confess to disheartened gaffer, being mature (5,2)
24 Verbal attacks when bride is at work (9)
25 Judged to be exhausted, having run back (5)
26 Make an enquiry after tense undertaking (4)
27 Stage magician fills pit worker with fear (4,6)

Down

1 One thousand and one cooking hobs to spoil (6)
2 Deny Lonsdale belts are something to wear (6)
3 They certainly see lots of people! (7,7)
4 Asking her out might mean a loss of business! (9)
5 Regret never having returned to register (5)
7 Locate smells and find remedies, possibly (8)
8 Points South – that's hardly necessary (8)
9 Trouble with drink? Take it to bed! (3-5,6)
15 Reinvigorated on seeing red, perhaps (9)
16 Believe to be under a cloud at first, but provide certification (8)
17 Ignore note on girl with such an accent (3,5)
19 Relax after a French victory over Germany (6)

14

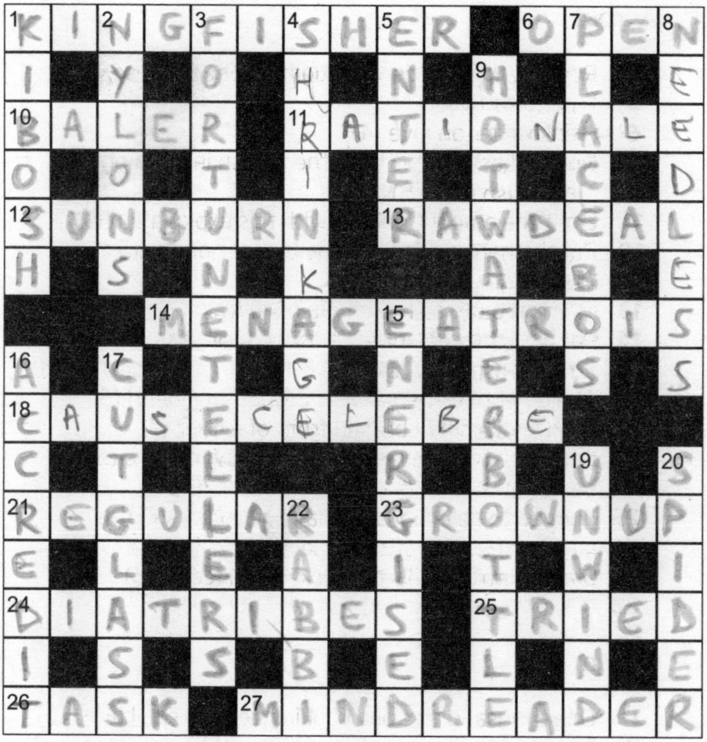

20 Rest the spinner (6)
22 Spiritual leader who might talk endlessly (5)

Across

1 Severely criticise a mother's hat (6)
5 What could make Meg stare - something under the stairs? (3,5)
9 It sounds as though you'll get wonderful wine from this book (10)
10 Two parties and the bird's dead! (4)
11 Sort of mammal seen in garden art gallery (8)
12 Regular girl left (6)
13 Court getting Duke to make deal? (4)
15 Old books in part accounting for revolution (8)
18 Bird makes new beginning around first of December (8)
19 At side of road behold peer (4)
21 Sausage is black - great displeasure! (6)
23 Secret on film not yet developed? (2,6)
25 Keep out of sight in old area of land (4)
26 Transferrence of power finally effected a sort of change (10)
27 One making proposal could be more gentle (8)
28 Walks unnaturally in street with potholes (6)

Down

2 Change commercial to get blokes in (5)
3 Elements playin' a part on fateful day (9)
4 One making cuts in the forestry business? (6)
5 Gentle Rover in struggle with dire dog (6,9)
6 Terribly inert, yes, in a state of peace (8)
7 Duck 'one ding or dee udder'! (5)
8 Try to get the name of Cook's ship (9)
14 Labourer ever messing about with patio (9)
16 Wobble when holding lunar module's scientific instrument (9)
17 Dog in lake abroad, swimming (Rex) (8)
20 Weighs plates (6)

15

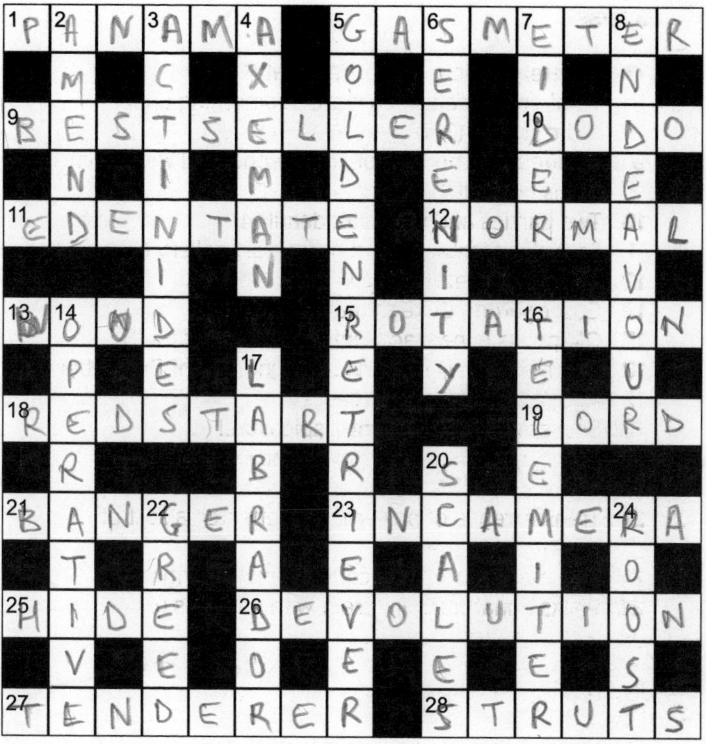

22 Undertook to ignore a bad sort of desire (5)
24 Shelter in kangaroo's territory (5)

Across

1 Queen to disappear going round overcome (8)
6 Champion setter perhaps (3,3)
9 Way to go round on leisurely walk (6)
10 Obstinate train driver? (8)
11 Food Mario can prepare (8)
12 Sophy, sickly child, consumed some medicine (6)
13 Before thought it had been planned in advance (12)
16 It comes at the end of a four-week period (6-6)
19 The man caught in charge rushed (6)
21 Nora paid stranger having irrational fears (8)
23 A game with US soldier having advance defence (8)
24 Grant immunity to former Euro member before time (6)
25 A number in duplicate on shelter (6)
26 Wind, gusty, set in prematurely (8)

Down

2 Starry semicircular moulding Georgia left (6)
3 Audibly refer to a portion (5)
4 Part of Cambridgeshire, sounds like part of cathedral (4,2,3)
5 Border height that's worn? (7)
6 From a bulb this could be lit up (5)
7 Testy chap transferred money in the office (5,4)
8 Biased - could be wholly right (3-5)
13 Meticulous without you and me in strict observance of etiquette (9)
14 Working like a horse? (2,7)
15 We set about vegetable or flower (5,3)
17 I name spot where it has been positioned (2,5)
18 Drive away Diane's gymnastic pupil (6)
20 Lacey's partner in fighting crime losing point of being secretive (5)
22 Relative coming from place in France, it is heard (5)

16

The Telegraph

Across

1 Song that's naughty - everyone joins in! (6)
4 Heroic Greek units holding an elevated position (8)
9 Burning with fresh zeal after a bad start (6)
10 Girl in love getting married was subdued (8)
12 Spot the wimp (4)
13 Company about to declare capital (5)
14 Beat the unbeatable (4)
17 Packed garment for a self-important personage (7,5)
20 Disc jockey's abbreviated clothing (6,6)
23 Slough outbuilding (4)
24 A salesman's pitch (5)
25 Games room (4)
28 Home to have pride in (5,3)
29 Show great respect for returning Chinese vessel - a tug (6)
30 Cast my anchor in Norway, say (8)
31 Sea air (6)

Down

1 Flourish a cereal bowl (8)
2 Its population was literally very small (8)
3 Commercials, we hear, for a woodcutter (4)
5 They don't pay for food or drink in restaurants (5,7)
6 With reference to having free rein (2,2)
7 The instruction he gets will be brief (6)
8 Teased about being placid (6)
11 Chap seemed in trouble in debut as an M.P. (6,6)
15 Join in a very loud number (5)
16 It was ground in the gutter (5)
18 Framework keels over with added weight (8)
19 Don't come, but give support elsewhere (4,4)
21 Refuge a youth originally found in squat (6)
22 Leading lady cut short with smack (6)

17

26 A good man rises to king and emperor (4)
27 Leave and say nothing? My word! (4)

Across

1 State where girl is sanctimonious about small drink (11)
9 Winner woman snubbed for glamorous drink (9)
10 Some unofficial on-goings in company (5)
11 Take in popular tipple around hotel (6)
12 Setback with exhibit swamping Royal Society (8)
13 Flatterer gaining attention with judge (6)
15 Fellow of no practical importance (8)
18 Very clever chap getting support at home before case (8)
19 Love song again appearing in middle of date (6)
21 Irritating remote is malfunctioning (8)
23 Call for more action on boards? (6)
26 Hunt missing leader, a swift seeker of prey? (5)
27 Distinct delight after time with queen (9)
28 Dogmatic medical figure? One detained by agitated trainer (11)

Down

1 Scot with joint, not good? Artificial device needed (7)
2 Cut first sign of laziness in band (5)
3 It drives mischief-maker and soul in play (9)
4 One that's wise to contemplate – not half! (4)
5 Affected manner disrupting centre in exercises (8)
6 Stupid lot in China needlessly (5)
7 Beautiful plant pruned (7)
8 Light backing for service held by energetic figure (8)
14 Aggression in an estate after a scrape? (4,4)
16 Native Caribbean brother? (9)
17 Superficially attractive item vaguely caught south of island (8)
18 Cell where eggs are found? (7)
20 Revolutionary officer among wild trees getting support (7)

18

22 Drug that's positive in origin (5)
24 African native certainly followed by an investigator (5)
25 Tackle illicit drugs (4)

Across

8 Fruit repeatedly said to produce disease in East (8)
9 Secure position as TV presenter (6)
10 What divides opponents in court is clear (3)
11 For projection, put up too many pictures? (8)
12 One's repelled by disgusted reaction – no more! (6)
13 Not above board? (5,3,7)
15 Barge carrying less weight (7)
18 Flower that we finally got out of bed (3,4)
21 As entertaining TV, it has its place (9,6)
24 Mad Hatter's aggressive statement (6)
25 During fourth period of play, England opener's sluggish (8)
26 Removed from menu, having gone bad (3)
27 Go for fix (6)
28 For example, good leaders can be so-called intellectuals (8)

Down

1 Don't accept new cause of ferment (6)
2 Cut portion without right (6)
3 In parts of France, rent a large shop (10,5)
4 One-time athlete's garment (7)
5 They allow currency conversion and charge fees, no tax involved (5,2,8)
6 Glass vessel (8)
7 Party for some Indians in American houses (8)
14 Boxer, perhaps, whose chance is non-existent (3)
16 They include one's husband and another male in Erin, possibly (8)
17 Poet's pronouncement for doctor (8)
19 Be expected to give back love to partners (3)
20 Fir cone could be produced by one (7)

19

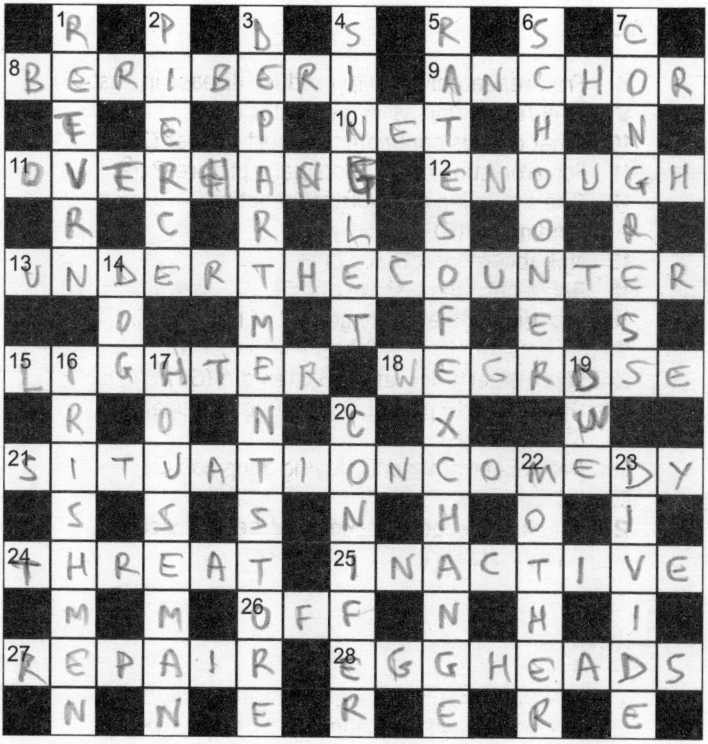

22 Little boy's brought up by her (6)
23 Separate old coin, I see (6)

Across

7 How Jaguar fought with Rover? (3-3-3)
8 What is held as true could also be the reverse (5)
10 Shop soiled bouquet one accepted (8)
11 Drink rackets (6)
12 Midwives have a lot of time for this girl (4)
13 Good! Fish, fish and fish (8)
16 Pitch black? (4)
18 One might follow his advice, of course, and lose (7)
20 Sport dealing with hot goods (7)
22 International examination? (4)
24 Doctor with broken nails a picture! (4,4)
26 Possesses heroin and marijuana (4)
29 Iron man showing characteristics of the opposite sex (6)
30 Harsh pace, and not disheartened (8)
31 Manoeuvre always on the road (5)
32 Payments owing links to the crown? (9)

Down

1 Cards that are, thank you very much, rubbish (5)
2 Lawsuit about empty theatrical building (6)
3 A day to correspond will be enough (8)
4 Strange rule in support of a government department (7)
5 Engineers the people into a form of government (8)
6 One signs a release for timber treatment (9)
9 Part of the planet that is rising, swamped by motorists (4)
14 Half fare, initially for Sunday match officials (4)
15 Eire put to flight and in a spin (9)
17 Leftovers in short supply! (4)
19 Sailor putting the food in – to burn! (8)
21 Very light ale brewed over in that place (8)
23 To share is possible, if in range (7)
25 Team's leader travels South for a day in Rome (4)

20

27 Calm corner of England before engagement (6)
28 The darling finally changed sides in fury (5)

[PANASONIC VAC BELT]

Across

1 Like certain politics represented in comedic art (10)
6 Has boor to collect this? Looks like it! (4)
9 Favourite pupil's first to get testimonial (10)
10 The man with an explosive laugh (2-2)
12 Girl on Aussie truck gets greeting (6)
13 Deal with riot stirred up by primitive worshipper? (8)
15 One thing put up so that other things can be 'decreased'? (7,5)
18 Players in company wearing some underwear (12)
21 Polite Scot, not one of the soldiers (8)
22 Entrance opened by the French ambassador (6)
24 Kind maiden given lyrical words (4)
25 Unlikely to get out (4-2-4)
26 Make a mistake ending in some knot (4)
27 Ridiculously vile ranter not worth bothering about (10)

Down

1 Dismiss model after journalist's been upset (6)
2 Food miles needing to be modified will involve you ultimately (6)
3 See what may be green or brown item of furniture (12)
4 Some babe dozing in cot? (4)
5 Client and I becoming entangled by chance (10)
7 Ghastly carpets thrown out and left (8)
8 Rule against sweetheart heading off on journey (8)
11 Be altogether excited in old playhouse (5,7)
14 Man participating in a talk that's of interest to physicists (10)
16 Put label on headgear going up with astronaut (8)
17 Allowing that to be supplied (8)
19 Man very large having a piece of fried food (6)
20 Modern church brought in money from property (6)
23 Instrument contributing to jollly rehearsal (4)

1 D	E	2 M	O	3 C	R	4 A	T	5 I	C	■	6 A	7 S	B	8 O
E	■	U	■	H	■	B	■	N	■	■	■	P	■	V
9 P	R	E	F	E	R	E	N	C	E	■	10 H	E	H	E
O	■	S	■	S	■	D	■	I	■	11 G	■	C	■	R
12 S	A	L	U	T	E	■	13 I	D	O	L	A	T	E	R
E	■	I	■	E	■	14 A	■	E	■	O	■	R	■	I
■	■	■	15 I	R	O	N	I	N	G	B	O	A	R	D
16 S	■	17 P	■	F	■	T	■	T	■	E	■	L	■	E
18 P	A	R	T	I	C	I	P	A	N	T	S	■	■	■
A	■	O	■	E	■	M	■	L	■	H	■	19 S	■	20 R
21 C	I	V	I	L	I	A	N	■	22 L	E	G	A	T	E
E	■	I	■	D	■	T	■	23 L	■	A	■	M	■	C
24 M	O	D	E	■	25 S	T	A	Y	A	T	H	O	M	E
A	■	E	■	■	■	E	■	R	■	R	■	S	■	N
26 N	O	D	E	■	27 I	R	R	E	L	E	V	A	N	T

Across

1 Novel thing to cover the drink (8)
9 Unconscious in a horizontal position distant from main area (8)
10 List first 18 letters back to front (4)
11 Lady has prize fruit (8,4)
13 Notes it's becoming the hardest (8)
15 Georgia's note on Frenchman (6)
16 Attempt to include a salver (4)
17 Poem finished put away (3,2)
18 Fish, most unappetising part (4)
20 Distress? (6)
21 Ingenious to include four, then one more at birth (8)
23 Disinterest caused by situation of not having a catalogue? (12)
26 Top worker in the cake industry (4)
27 Nothing replaces one during holiday job (8)
28 Would one make a fresh cuppa with it? (5,3)

Down

2 Devoted admirer who declares he is a procrastinator (8)
3 Very many angels or just St. Peter? (8,4)
4 Timekeeper, not Kelvin, he had cover for plants (6)
5 To a small degree musical (4)
6 Hang cord in a higher place (6,2)
7 Girl shortly having a breather (4)
8 First person with illness suffering morbid self-confidence (8)
12 Definite indication of a plus? (8,4)
14 Notary struggling loses article in bold bid (3-2)
16 Right-o darling (8)
17 Great area of liquidity (4,4)
19 Observe what follows when none beat a retreat (4,4)
22 Chance for a singer? (6)

22

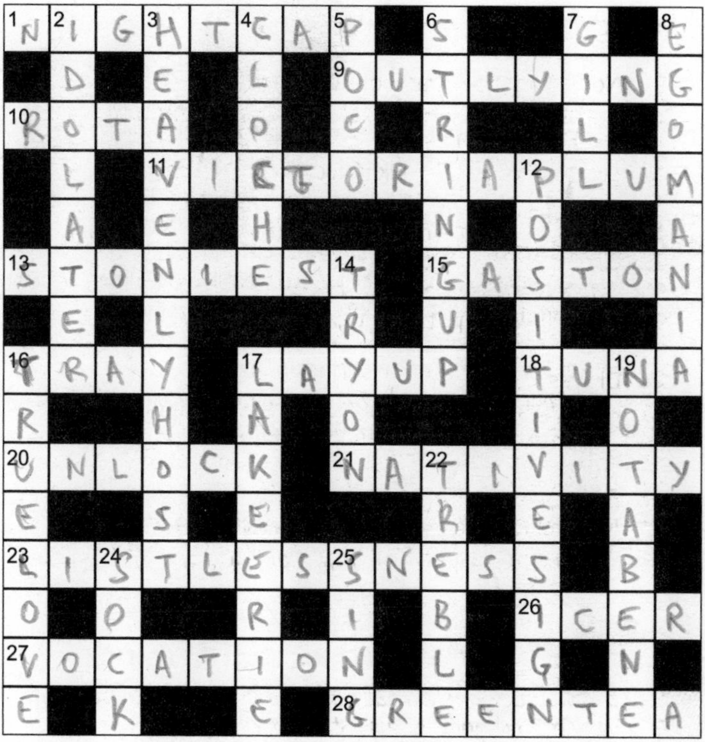

24 Blow back? (4)
25 Char stopped short to make notes (4)

Across

7 Roundly curse a set of pruning shears (9)
8 A Greek style (5)
10 Hole-in-the-middle mint (5-3)
11 Rows with sweetheart are not frequent (6)
12 Macho boss (4)
13 Close of play (8)
15 Restricts Christmas food consignments (7)
17 He gains nothing but pleasure from his activities (7)
20 It provides a lift for those wanting to go up (8)
22 Novice leads expert in tie (4)
25 Kept self-sufficient by a sum of petty cash (6)
26 Magician demonstrates trick to member of a panel (8)
27 Used by pilots – for levelling out? (5)
28 Drink at ball game (9)

Down

1 It's rolled up for the opening (5)
2 Vote to return to the dance (6)
3 Challenged champion's delay about the final (8)
4 Arranged, but not voluntary (7)
5 Leave with a clip around the ear (5,3)
6 He's coming in to sign reference book (9)
9 It's a rum drink (4)
14 Precipitate drop of current – flaw later rectified (9)
16 Put the case against the euro (8)
18 Italians seal mine after explosion (8)
19 Parties appeal to him (7)
21 One shouldn't lie under it (4)
23 He could get his work done by Friday (6)
24 Just a little finger (5)

23

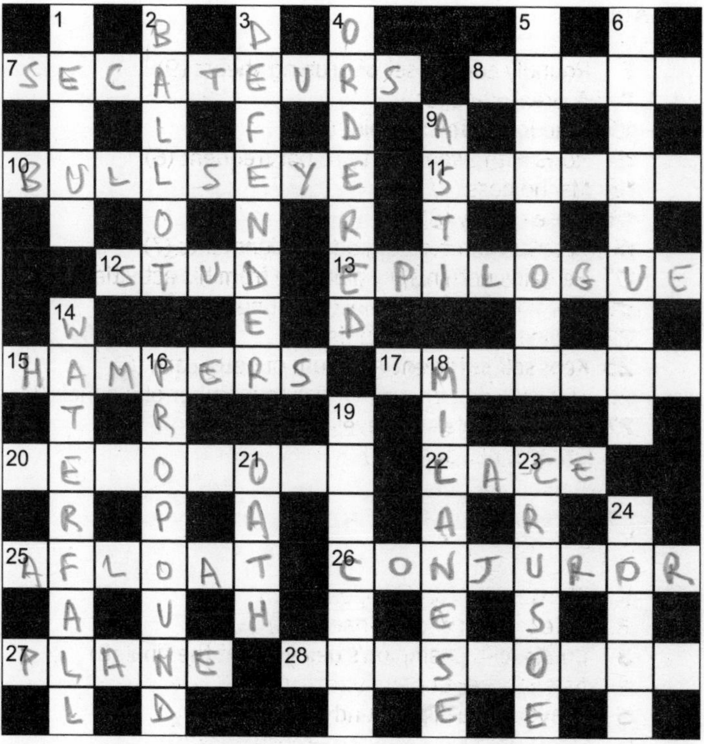

Across

1 Law, say, is changed for good (6)
5 Bottle up seeing journalists on drink (8)
9 Pretend to be ill? Stay with mum (8)
10 Execute right after criminal's bird (6)
11 Fine end of April in rustic surroundings (8)
12 Nervous and pale losing heart (6)
13 Liberal queen taking anything for amusement (8)
15 'I will shortly...', we hear, for Innisfree? (4)
17 Initially revealed on performing execution (4)
19 Drop iron? (8)
20 Second coffee before mid-afternoon (6)
21 Unruly teen with gaol stretch (8)
22 Boss chasing Middle Eastern support (6)
23 Interesting new leader admits a bad start (8)
24 Sign on in Bognor Regis? Terrific (8)
25 Judge faces reversal on end of sentence (6)

Down

2 Terrible fall sees trees like this (8)
3 Civil and warm - cold inside (8)
4 Get Iran upset with US endorsement (9)
5 Supporter of the NHS? (9-6)
6 Landing includes solitary colonist (7)
7 Place loaded, possibly, containing gold (8)
8 Choirboy's clothing not necessary, say! (8)
14 Tortuous English and American work finished (9)
15 Admirer's one-party following (8)
16 Look over an object of hatred (8)
17 Star of 'Dragnet', I fancy (3,5)
18 Sweet secretary, sedentary sweetheart (8)
19 Dredges river locks (7)

24

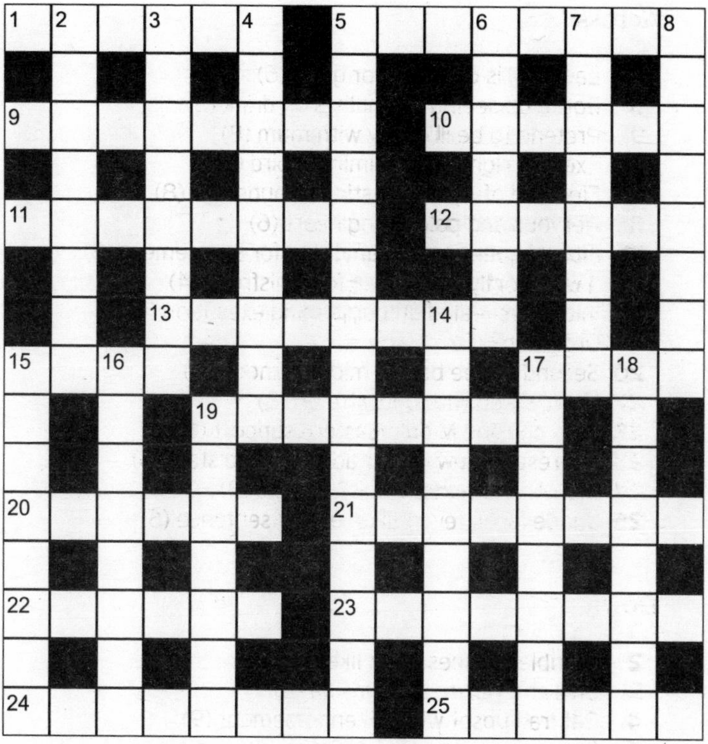

Across

- **7** Established trades put in dire position (7,2)
- **8** Prepare to fire first (5)
- **10** Note leading actor takes the fewest things possible (6)
- **11** Herb is awfully arrogant (8)
- **12** Poor singer wants to pack it in (6)
- **14** Rather good-looking (6)
- **16** Fail to answer, yet be successful (4)
- **17** Some of the grease we removed from the drain (5)
- **18** Heavyweights in abundance (4)
- **19** Hit by small cycle (6)
- **21** Colour of a corn-fed chicken? (6)
- **24** They shoot large fish (8)
- **26** German weapon made of shiny metal (6)
- **27** The more macho of two males,maybe (2-3)
- **28** Chatters away whilst top conductor's performing (7,2)

Down

- **1** Divest oneself of football gear (5)
- **2** Easter display includes popular students (8)
- **3** Asian in Alpine resort (6)
- **4** Clothing worn in clubs, maybe (4)
- **5** A monarch may meet oriental in secret (6)
- **6** I'm left with a worker of significance (9)
- **9** Professional salesman retired, as is right (6)
- **13** Present all the time? Absolutely not! (2,3)
- **15** Saving dinghy for local worker (9)
- **17** Given directions to garden in the country (6)
- **18** As duplicitous as Janus (3-5)
- **20** Acting for fun (2,4)
- **22** The French entrance an emissary (6)
- **23** Exclusive kitchen tool (5)
- **25** Scotsman is upset by fraud (4)

25

Across

7 Run into Ms Davis and Ms Taylor, perhaps (8)
9 Disturbance caused by father when ringing around (6)
10 Naughty child, last to admit mistake (6)
11 Messy hit-and-run? (8)
12 A cabby can manage without his tips (4-4,6)
15 Cold shoulder and rolls sent back (4)
17 Love some, but not all, abstract paintings (2,3)
19 Head of enquiry on free trip (4)
20 Film barrister attending meeting (5,9)
23 Ship's hands initially wearing new 2s (5,3)
25 Splendid gathering happy to be shown round LA Times? (6)
27 Healthy number taking in Montreal's centre (6)
28 General, one working in former SA province (8)

Down

1 Release without charge (4)
2 A girl, on far side of deck, in a waterproof jacket (6)
3 Part of the barracks in an untidy state (4)
4 A female, impartial in business (6)
5 Transfer of diamonds in German city (4,4)
6 Musical chairs at first? Earl'd organised this game (4,6)
8 Fuss about rep breaking weapon (7)
13 Banter? None, unfortunately, with novelist (4,6)
14 Artist brought in can teach (5)
16 Book on trendy English resort (8)
18 A concept, however ahead of time (7)
21 Projecting piece left in tooth close to canine (6)
22 Admiral in hold (6)
24 Considerate type (4)
26 Photograph ten fish (1-3)

26

Across

1 Hurried to get hold of Bill (not in huddle) (6)
5 Wise man hugging me on the street in term-time (8)
9 Forging alibi with 'a cold' - wicked! (10)
10 Close in almost complete darkness (4)
11 Rascal observed going round China with Penny (8)
12 Rebels when Religious Education has book of Bible (6)
13 Liberated female about to take drug (4)
15 A ship said to be resting in the water (2,6)
18 A threesome trashing one big town in appalling act (8)
19 Someone who's been given an honour, look! (4)
21 Agent returning to river in van (6)
23 Plans to have school punishment dismissed originally (8)
25 Some hit - magnificent old show! (4)
26 When disturbed, dreamy bore becomes abrasive (5,5)
27 Cheer up when a holiday resort is mentioned (8)
28 Give time for number to get back in (6)

Down

2 Dress fussily in skirt that's very soft on the outside (5)
3 Spanish gent about to join dance - 'erculean fellow (9)
4 US diplomat most boring, unable to reach conclusion (6)
5 No nerdy comrades will be able to mix in school (9,6)
6 Abuse - awful matter involving a learner (8)
7 Girl's churning over - it's the laxative (5)
8 I get homes sorted out for four couples maybe (9)
14 About to meet vehicle in country lane? One pulls back (9)
16 Goat gets crop on south of the island (9)
17 Most angry if tree is destroyed (8)
20 Went off course - not right, you should have waited! (6)
22 Accident puts Rex in pain (5)
24 Bird landing finally in tree after flying (5)

27

Across

1 Almost stuck with firm plaster (6)
4 Track left in the snow perhaps (8)
10 Constructive member of society? (5)
11 Nearby the broken biscuit (9)
12 Unconventional start in passage (7)
13 Bloke at liberty to precede privileged citizen (7)
14 Celebrate very late, create a new thing from personal magnetism (4,1,5,2,2)
17 Motorist surprisingly said to be free from accidents (8,6)
21 Left silver in central boss of a shield – it's a pain (7)
23 Art's follower has curious propriety (7)
24 Teacher has the answer – it will open many doors (6-3)
25 Doesn't sound like a warm country (5)
26 Cut short a few feet where ships are repaired and maintained (8)
27 Place each name inside ground kernel (6)

Down

1 Formerly an unspecified period (8)
2 Each slunk over when set free (9)
3 May a man of virtue have a game of cards? (7)
5 1 down in the past presumably when everything went wrong (3,2,5,4)
6 Fruit removed from goal net (7)
7 Thomas accepted half of tent pole (5)
8 Being punished for settling a debt! (6)
9 One who is not fully employed (4-4,6)
15 Change of position in the story (9)
16 Fourth strange knock at rub-a-dub-dub (8)
18 Card's dishonesty (7)
19 Use again after processing celery about to be included (7)

28

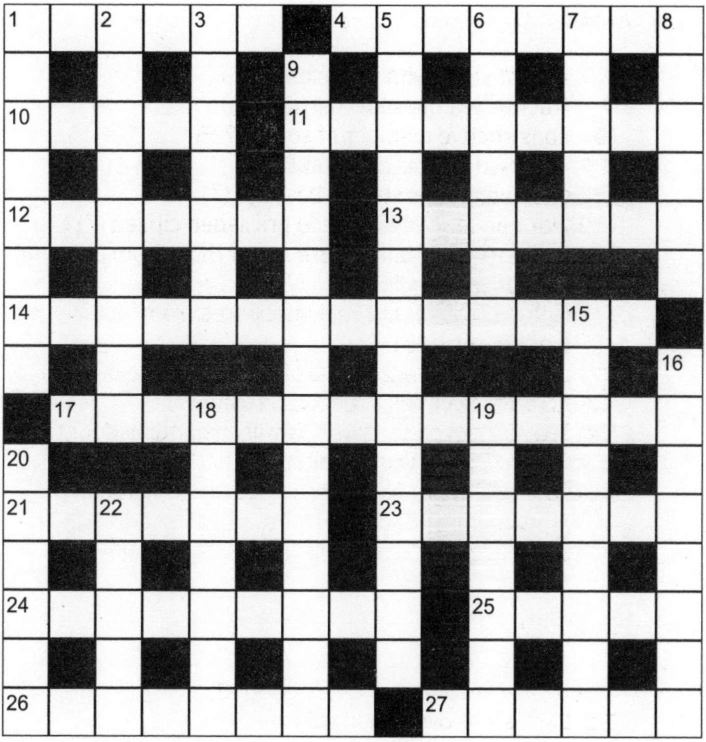

20 Found fault with Edward having cooked lamb first (6)
22 Greek character thus in harmony (5)

Across

1 Priest altered position in campaign (6)
5 Wine and beer around college? It provides good feeling (8)
9 Reflective type that sticks out on estate? (4,6)
10 Resist lively young man (4)
11 Some wag possibly inspiring hot TV programme (4,4)
12 Recommending timeless trip (6)
13 Principal disheartened fellow devising courses (4)
15 Sister church hiding where money's saved – source of trouble? (8)
18 Something discharged at home in news report (8)
19 Supporter trapped by tall youth (4)
21 A lawyer holding the latest plan for meeting (6)
23 An arty view in the main? (8)
25 Reportedly trim couple (4)
26 Discordant organ in pad? Not this instrument! (5,5)
27 A singular political body banning a Democrat? It's given nod (8)
28 Copper, we hear, showing nerve (6)

Down

2 Island's northerly capital importing trade (5)
3 Contrite man with fur let off (9)
4 Parking by worthless hole (6)
5 Drunk in loo beginning to surrender control and give up (5,2,4,4)
6 Company in train sadly cold and inducing sleep (8)
7 A couple of bishops overlooking holy books for religious leader (5)
8 Brief toss of a coin – call! (9)
14 Slim-waisted girl supporting greedy chap around old city (9)
16 New stain besetting leading supporter of disorder (9)

29

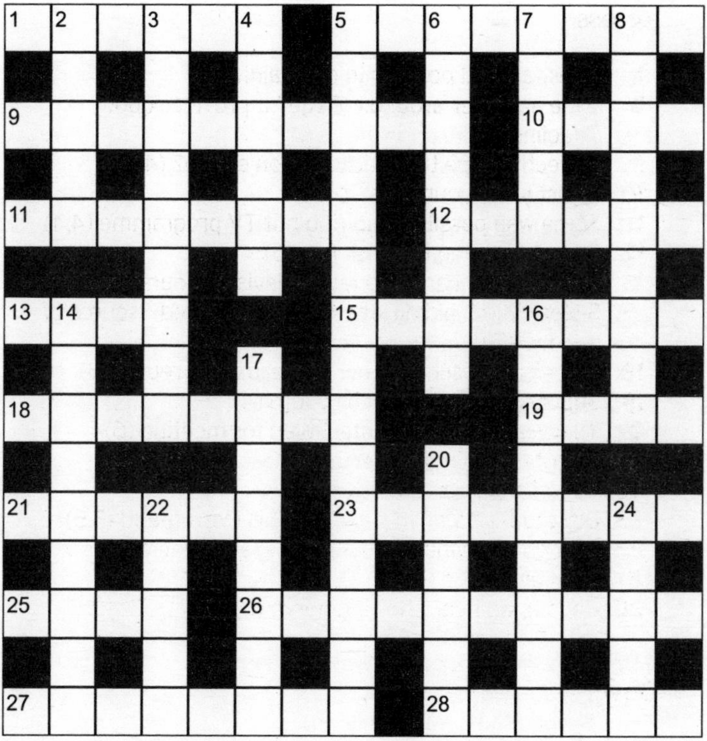

17 Normal maritime passage in broadcast (8)
20 Irregular matter (and ominous partly) (6)
22 Bring up sister? (5)
24 Very severe writer, a lecturer (5)

Across

7 Smooth Blair cut apart by English (9)
8 Firm carrying old stock (5)
10 In slander I detect insult (6)
11 Fish on grand stream for fish (8)
12 Censored strip, say (6)
14 Moderately left in Labour, for example (6)
16 Ceremony is just for the audience (4)
17 Commotion with sailors on deck (5)
18 Hamlet? Desperate character joining sweetheart (4)
19 Contradict female intuition (6)
21 Aspen is fashionable, not posh (6)
24 Dad's tastes for tarts (8)
26 One's on top of the world! (6)
27 Vacuous row about Labour leader (5)
28 Agreed on a cocktail for drink (9)

Down

1 Still, stop taking Ecstasy (5)
2 Watering can, possibly (8)
3 Vet show on television (6)
4 Second title's 'Men Only' (4)
5 Blimey! The French right's more fashionable (6)
6 Does my bum look big in this? (9)
9 A politician in retreat's wet (6)
13 Fall down dead with bad back (5)
15 Blair seems endlessly, terribly wretched (9)
17 A fine, fine romance (6)
18 Debate is turning into disorder (8)
20 Voice of No. Ten, I fancy (6)
22 Bush, perhaps admitting Iran's first yielding (6)
23 Woods' man with woods? (5)
25 Silky and radiant, Indian initially (4)

30

Across

1 Checking car travel round Ulster (10)
6 Trendy headgear back in the States (4)
9 Toddler gets a pound, but that's the lot (5)
10 A comedian playing in Europe (9)
12 Fellow-soldier aids Mr Cameron, maybe (7-2-4)
14 Embarrassed as Socialist gets confronted (3-5)
15 Not so light; not so bright (6)
17 Capital decoration for English couple in Oz (6)
19 Arab guide sees parent in monster's clutches (8)
21 If you receive this, you'll understand (3,3,7)
24 Don't bother about Mervin and Ned (5,4)
25 In the past it helped the church survive (5)
26 Included in Gore's circle as well (4)
27 Look in after offer is undercut (10)

Down

1 Gospel writer showing little polish (4)
2 Observed Bill and daughter (7)
3 Go on! One story's not enough! (4,2,7)
4 Rooted round as said spirit matured (8)
5 Find Henry in lovely little corner (5)
7 Puzzle how to beat lightweight (7)
8 Boss determined to be wilful (10)
11 He takes steps to instruct his charges (7,6)
13 Really good look expressly to find misleading information (10)
16 Took the chair, despite having shown earlier bias (8)
18 Reasons why I have put in French words (7)
20 Most are moved by his fine playing (7)
22 I entered warren carrying cereal (5)
23 Humble yet miserly (4)

31

Across

1 Burning to see South American climbdown (12)
9 How many riding crossed the motorway at under twenty? (7)
10 An obligation when returning for fruit (7)
11 City from which manservant comes back before four (3,4)
12 Richard accepts mistake in lifting gear (7)
13 Fashion news oddly peters out (5)
14 Sunshine falls on top of this army accommodation (6,3)
16 Punished, the way one is in being pursued (9)
19 Stamp, as taken in part fare (5)
21 Subjects encompassing river zones (7)
23 Doubled up after credit was relaxed! (7)
24 Love to put a limit on speech (7)
25 European – Russian – leader went missing (7)
26 Leaving the business when it's successful? (5,7)

Down

1 One male, white, died transfixed (7)
2 Splits from Conservatives and goes (7)
3 Nary a one with openings – what anticlimaxes! (3-6)
4 Relieved when sunk in rising river (5)
5 Gathering litter on lake (7)
6 Feed for hours in panic (7)
7 The rationale merely provided one with plan of action (13)
8 Sell beds in these places? No, just fruit and veg (6-7)
15 Winning love, but teaching without heart to support son (9)
17 A very old bounder, old fruit! (7)
18 Instruction for knowing instinctively, without being fashionable (7)
19 Take the lead prior to surrender (7)

32

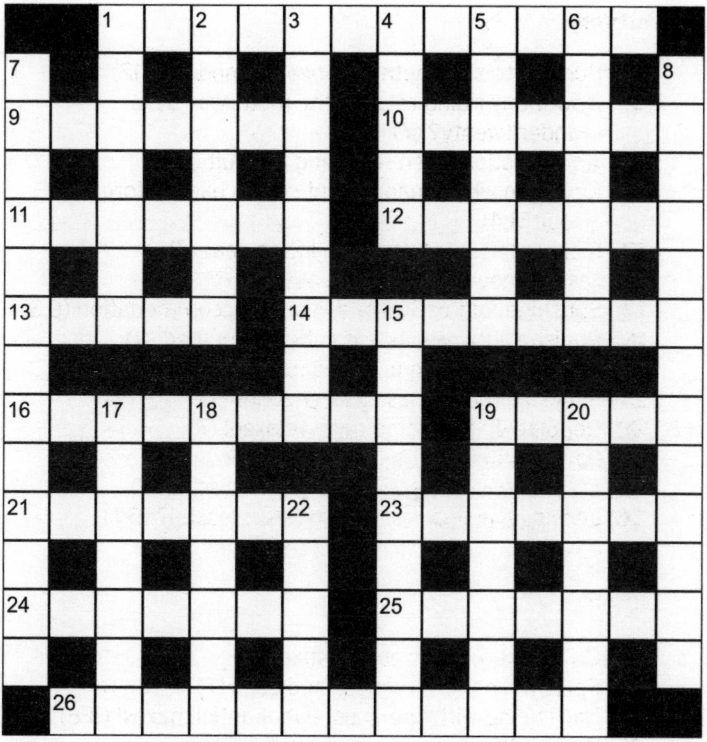

20 A term for jam, for example (7)
22 Working inside thus produces a boom of sorts (5)

Across

1 What may restrict Polly's walk in London (8)
5 Exclamation in school when there's roast (6)
9 Heartlessly capture many a whale (8)
10 Not much food and drink consumed by American broadcasters (6)
12 I must rail about undue emphasis on ceremony (9)
13 Only half spoil child? No (5)
14 Institution with church highly decorated (4)
16 Good to everyone, little creature being brave (7)
19 Natural covering fruit gets with time (7)
21 Caused to be insane before end of life (4)
24 Indian state in which Derek's given greeting (5)
25 A crowd outwardly ecstatic in religious ceremony (9)
27 Model given ridicule at university (4-2)
28 Extra sum at school? (8)
29 Isn't Queen able to move at a gentle pace? (6)
30 Like a football match using the entire pitch throughout (3-2-3)

Down

1 White powder in piece of cloth vehicle carries around (6)
2 Speak in ceremony outside city (6)
3 Girl dressed inadequately, artist (5)
4 Sentimentality over attractive person not all that wonderful (7)
6 Dog followed and cut short (9)
7 Tree in Burma exceptionally brown (8)
8 She and I organised gallery stall (8)
11 Pollution with sulphur getting elder statesman upset (4)
15 I troubled mine aunt before very long (2,1,6)
17 Disease got by daughter tucking into pie mice fouled up (8)
18 Man behind bars? (8)

33

20 Some see a star and point (4)
21 Academic club first appearing in old kingdom (7)
22 Settle three-quarters of the plan at the end of the month (6)
23 Saint – one died, being this (6)
26 Like a top event restricted by fundmentalists (1-4)

Across

1 Favourite in form (8,3)
9 A carrier I included of birds (5)
10 Lager's not mixed to make other beer (6,3)
11 Informal gift (7)
12 Valerie and Harry went to Los Angeles place of bliss (8)
14 Georgia, last character preparing a chop and soup (8)
15 Young lady, novice, had dope (4)
17 Having recovered using phrase to preface comments (4,3)
19 River port has not been finished (4)
20 Turn repeatedly to west and north and behave unrestrainedly (2,2,4)
21 Contentment of grand young fellow by loch (8)
23 Marched on this ground at start of day (7)
25 Doing away with former pupil through sound (9)
26 Animal entered many a large enclosure (5)
27 Opening car window when relaxing (7,4)

Down

2 More run (5)
3 Garments put on a horse? (7)
4 Encourages vermin on utensil (3-5)
5 Look up and down (4)
6 Sit down for one of the services (4,1,3)
7 Plucky way of dealing with notes (9)
8 Monks are given instructions (5,6)
12 Area of liquidity in a small place (7,4)
13 Gag Noel performing lasting a considerable time (3-4)
16 Misleadingly a tailor's right to be included, it is to do with him (9)
17 Retract whilst in possession of tie (8)
18 Offering job not starting before getting the Parisian into trouble (8)
19 Pointed out new books appearing in the act (7)

34

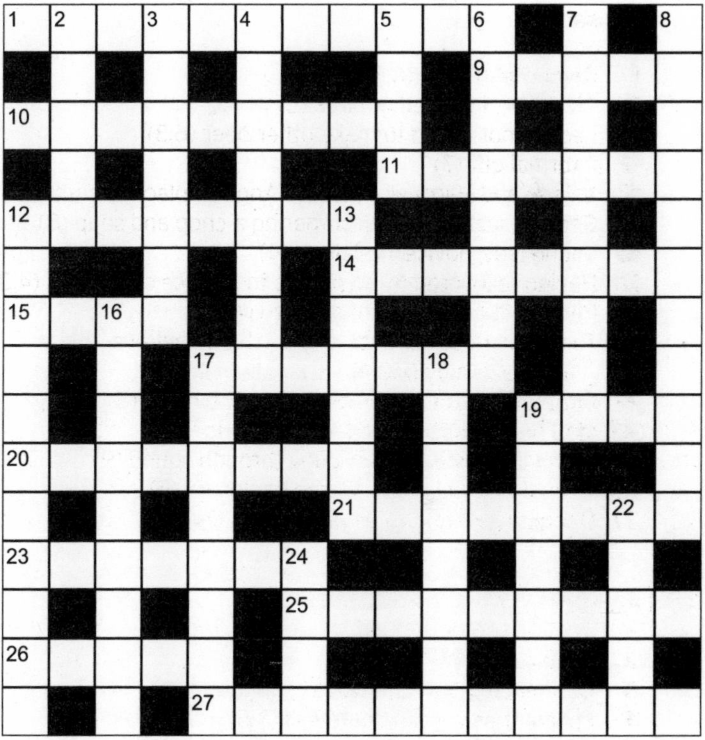

22 One going in all directions for fibrous tissue (5)
24 Performing no end of murder (2,2)

Across

1 Let priest go to remove mischievous spirit (11)
9 Revolver may be used when approaching big game (9)
10 Get used to being in old city quarter (5)
11 Songs the first violinist heard? (6)
12 Fighters engaged in shadow boxing (8)
13 Wear a well-styled beard (6)
15 The bits one pinches (8)
18 Scrap area where ships are built in Hong Kong? (8)
19 Horse and trap showing sign of neglect (6)
21 Recognise a criminal perhaps, but deny it if pushed (8)
23 To draw out English capital is O.K. in law (6)
26 Give out centre part of text due for revision (5)
27 Is in better position to make up (9)
28 Sadly lost the wind, it is very light (11)

Down

1 Two girls, one on each knee (7)
2 We don't want the criminal to be at it (5)
3 Fast finish (6,3)
4 Smile at the end of a Wagnerian opera (4)
5 Heading for the frozen wastes – or stuck in them (3-5)
6 He's taken to be a criminal (5)
7 Tributes to the dead from the wars (7)
8 Stop in front of a humble building (8)
14 Blue, perhaps, at university who never gets a first (6-2)
16 Not hampered by tight shoes? (9)
17 Soldier held to be healthy after service, but the writing is on the wall (8)
18 Carpenters likely to become members of a union? (7)
20 One bird pecked another (7)
22 Lifting the foot (5)
24 The atmosphere in a small firm may be capital (5)
25 Ends up in front of the old range (4)

35

Across

7 Common sort joining socialist (7)
8 Where deal may be cut? (7)
10 Reserve squad (10)
11 European cow, perhaps, producing cheese (4)
12 Press sink English party (8)
14 Lie from dishonest leader (6)
15 Working out grids, novice exploded (11)
19 Couple on about service (6)
20 Grabbing fish on line (8)
22 Horror of Tory head chasing support (4)
23 Carol, happy changing, getting made-up (10)
25 With chance to bat after appealing (7)
26 Magician's struggle with chain (7)

Down

1 It's dull beside the seaside, we hear (7)
2 Almost perfect clue (4)
3 Grab the woman's bottom! (6)
4 Frog maybe, fixed flipping Frenchman (8)
5 Starchy prison meal's cooked (10)
6 Yielding, first pleading guilty (7)
9 Doubt it's right Iran vetoes resolution (11)
13 Vessel's giant waves in seawater (10)
16 The end for hangings? (8)
17 Retinue protecting Queen and country (7)
18 Conceive following one new birth (7)
21 Crikey! Right and left initially shut up (6)
24 Run and hide (4)

36

Across

1 Virtually on level pegging (2,4,2)
9 Former priest in disarray (8)
10 Fuss follows fellows following football (4)
11 Only place to store documents one by one (2,6,4)
13 Investigation about Home-Counties' principal (8)
15 Way to get money? Baloney! (6)
16 Old seamen take responsibility (4)
17 Long for King Charles to accept greeting (5)
18 Peter is not at risk (4)
20 In Trieste employees are treated with respect (6)
21 Make less food with little content (8)
23 Spurn tigress resolved to take financial control (5-7)
26 Song that told a story (4)
27 They carry injections for a thousand French hens (8)
28 Island in March is bliss (8)

Down

2 Slut accepts last rent review (8)
3 Not a private place to dine (8,4)
4 Activist takes two seconds to find vagrant (6)
5 Hurries back prior to revolution (4)
6 Drive out from a woman's home (8)
7 Identical notes sung by operatic heroine (4)
8 If you hear it, you'll wake up (8)
12 Doffs one's cap, then loses it (5,4,3)
14 Tried by former Foreign Secretary, they say (5)
16 Ploy Vera used to get ham (8)
17 Many a French friend has only an undergarment (8)
19 Fortress on secure headland (8)
22 Way to acquire sound property (6)
24 Enthralled by artillery exercises (4)
25 Rex takes snake out of grating (4)

37

Across

1 Design feature lacking a free counter (6)
4 Blackened and marked around the central heating (8)
9 Cut off additional beer to engender team spirit (6)
10 How one might view transparent material given to agent (8)
11 Shattered relic by opening chamber (9)
13 Free time put into building toy for children (3,2)
14 Direct aircraft are noisy prior to reaching maximum altitude (5-8)
17 A doctrine is no substitute for careful reflection (13)
21 A look with feet in the air? (5)
23 The bursar is more certain to follow exchange rate (9)
24 This month start thinking about Irish police command (8)
25 Clever remark found on tomb in ruins (3,3)
26 Makes an effort and regularly baits with lures (8)
27 Tightens up when seeing perfect future in front of them! (6)

Down

1 Get rid of rage outside – hurry up! (6)
2 Striker to fix support for Formula One circuit (6,3)
3 Short story and opera song. Shoes by Hermes (7)
5 Police officer quietly delayed writing (11)
6 Like a monarch, one has a number of accoutrements (7)
7 Male with skill and courage (5)
8 Force out one's Labour leader in deceitful scheme (8)
12 Join snub about independent state (11)
15 Resign – or a muscle bound idiot will appear! (9)
16 A cause of pain, as a critic runs out in panic! (8)
18 Temporary home one found during school period (7)
19 Floundering – nor is he near the coast! (7)

38

20 Constant prices asked for old cars (6)
22 Working on radio is a beginning (5)

The Telegraph

Across

1 Move with speed? Have caution and a bit of hesitation (6)
4 A tonic possibly right for swallowing, cold drug (8)
8 Girls in specs? Not good! (6)
9 Urban dweller has slave after short time (8)
10 See group dynamic developing unconscious mechanism (8)
11 A female - feeble or on fire? (6)
12 Monitor army coming round to put paid to feud (8)
13 Pole about to join clique in the county (6)
15 Mister hugged by Dora, terrible disciplinarian (6)
18 Magnificent setting for a Duke University student about to collect degree (8)
20 Criminal pinching gold article - a bright ring (6)
21 Makes deflated, literally or figuratively (4,4)
23 Leaving out nothing at the start of letter (8)
24 Captain with cricket trousers only half on (6)
25 New hat style could be secret (8)
26 Time for a special dance? Help! (6)

Down

1 Phones everybody in the Civil Service (5)
2 Cockney festival with hidden aim (4-5)
3 Thoughtfulness shown by a minority of Yorkshire spectators (7)
4 A gaol internally repurposed as a building for works of art (8,7)
5 Man's dispute over territory (7)
6 I am drowned by awful blast from drums (7)
7 Happy prisoner in temporary accommodation? (9)
12 Woman beginning to cry 'I love America!' - and it's true (9)
14 Duo nearly wrecked song (9)

39

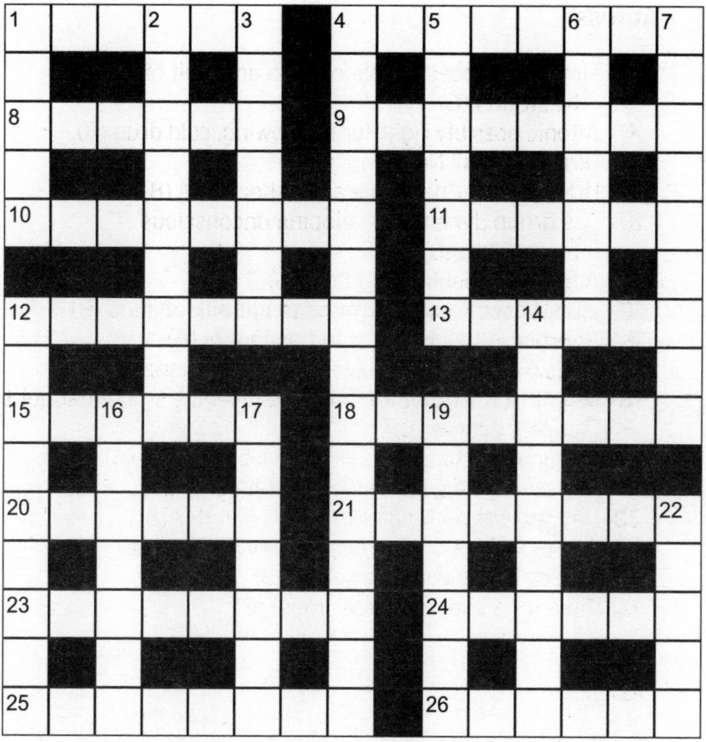

16 Skill needed to intercept explosive woman (7)
17 Nobody was such a writer (7)
19 Not many turning out to be the opposite (7)
22 Woman in New York is someone who'll look after the kids (5)

Across

2 They are not openly in force (6,6)
8 The two are not right in the soup (4)
9 Nigel ate revolting jelly-like food (8)
10 Burn something black or grey (8)
11 Small fish present after 30 seconds (6)
12 Be patient and we will find out, delay as Eden developed (4,3,3)
13 Vegetable stick inside shelter (6)
16 Beast used river before elevated railroad (5)
17 Coming from Mercia to the peninsula (6)
18 Tree used for making footwear? (10)
21 Express one's fear in alfresco play? (3,3)
23 Weighty seal almost coming out of ocean with big waves (5,3)
24 Astutely intriguing getting round MP (8)
25 Maiden's assistant? (4)
26 During time that one can remember explosive glimmer on ivy (6,6)

Down

1 Joseph's with Hugh heard to have taken a book (6)
2 Policy of long holidays? (5-4)
3 Softly murmur in study with silky envelope (6)
4 It certainly isn't a castle in Spain (11,4)
5 Confusedly both Papa and maiden receive short measure (4-4)
6 Reveal the Parisian fashion (3,2)
7 Many on river having soup (8)
14 Girl means to take horse to inlet in Ireland (6,3)
15 Rob suffering with colic from greens (8)
16 Movement on board moulding left inside (8)
19 Slowly in a noted way (6)

40

20 Go too far with exhaust (6)
22 Beast ruined biro containing first drop of ink (5)

Across

1 Magic Circle star? (8)
6 Promise the old man a part (6)
9 Pilot's error did the damage (6)
10 He has a home split round the side (8)
11 Study to invite scorn (8)
12 Scandinavian article in plate (6)
13 Carriage reserved for a small charge (12)
16 Disaffection of people in a Regent St riot (12)
19 Punishment in store? (6)
21 This plant requires proper drainage (8)
23 Exchange of gun-fire's declining (8)
24 Bob all set for musical party? (4-2)
25 Demon with extreme menace (6)
26 Team needs pace to avoid tackles (8)

Down

2 Take on work (6)
3 One asking for more tobacco perhaps (5)
4 A craft based on fundamental duplicity (9)
5 Mistake of deserter trapped by signs of hesitation (7)
6 Sat, when asked (5)
7 Surplus to requirements and turned off (9)
8 Cricketer yearns to be a spinner (4-4)
13 Air support for back-packers (9)
14 Found out such appliances are dangerous (9)
15 A hot line for the weather-man? (8)
17 Binds books (7)
18 Annoy a learned cleric, interrupting with a problem (6)
20 Reacted like a startled horse and threw (5)
22 Goes out of play (5)

41

Across

1 Hanging video's shot (8)
5 Holy man has a point on church policy (6)
9 Press one wavering to give answer (8)
10 Keep left in order (6)
12 Problem of retina? Yes, possibly (9)
13 Head of state on sorry track (5)
14 Practised with beer, holding bottle opener (4)
16 Missile's explosive contains free energy (7)
19 Oppressive old emperor's round the bend? (7)
21 Look both ways (4)
24 Change plug outside guys (5)
25 Troubled times in Blair's profession (9)
27 Labour with a new catchphrase (6)
28 Stucco covering one Roman column (8)
29 Smells of money, say (6)
30 Clergyman perpetually in split (8)

Down

1 Party struggles accepting ordinary leader (6)
2 More elegant puzzle, internally hard (6)
3 Game chap holding power (5)
4 'Express again?', others scoffed (7)
6 If partner is not straight, come out! (9)
7 Funny ring tone – it's a gas (8)
8 Curse former wife before end of divorce case (8)
11 Make outfit around top of needles? (4)
15 Bad actors ruined show (9)
17 It's sweet, thick girls chasing doctor (8)
18 Dash off and run off after girl (8)
20 Fill stomach and totally engorge, initially (4)
21 Setter's in fix for diversion (7)
22 Detest the French, embracing vulgarity (6)
23 In smithy, bride's cross (6)
26 Cross current with speed (5)

42

Across

1 Cryptic sign used by top civil servants (11)
7 Son gets sick at sea (7)
8 Acknowledged that soldiers worked steadily (7)
10 Astonished by display of charity (5)
11 Lake and river rose alarmingly (9)
12 Manage to make a woman accept Greek cross (7)
14 Mackerel have black eyes (7)
15 Entertainer takes time to redeem him (7)
18 Notes Italian city involved in boat production (7)
20 Oriel team resolved to improve (9)
21 The lady's upset by a laxative (5)
22 Praise a model plant (7)
23 Work set for every class (7)
24 Sound-system classified as standard (11)

Down

1 Chaps in dire need of food (7)
2 Agree to strike (5)
3 Awfully angered by swordsman's warning (2,5)
4 Stops giving detentions (7)
5 I am limited by being neutral (9)
6 Thorny column containing bone (7)
7 Thomas Yeats is distressed by unsociable people (4-2-5)
9 Challenges greeting in Tanzania (3,2,6)
13 Fancy getting English leftist to speak! (9)
16 Forays by Southern Confederates (7)
17 Issue makes oriental fellow fed up (7)
18 Tell reluctant miner to abandon shoddy cinema? (7)
19 Study rope-making in harmony (7)
21 Rob takes tour on Sunday (5)

43

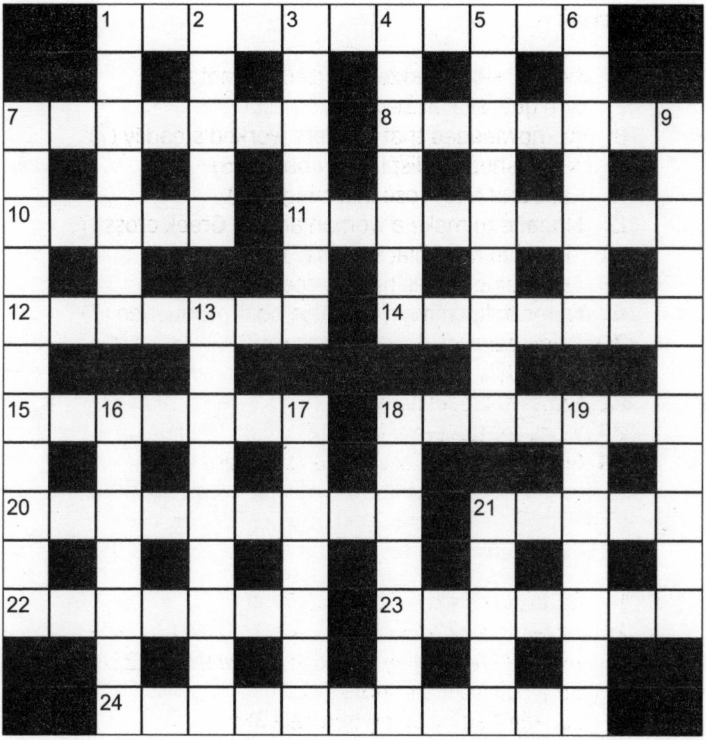

Across

1 Tolerating one's position in society (8)
5 Left back in charge, given latitude (6)
9 The province of a genuine Frenchman (5)
10 Material from which technical college had to steer away (9)
12 Hypnotised for a while before spring? (10)
13 The idiot on the lake should use it! (4)
15 Newspaper exposé on salts linked to disorder (4,3,4)
16 A runner from Hell's Kitchen? (3)
17 The day before is always short (3)
18 One won't drink and drive here – or tell at offending! (11)
20 Heroin in crack causes pain (4)
21 Limits are set covering one having to build up a fighting force (10)
24 Dust began to settle in a legislative assembly (9)
26 Helps to chase runs, and attacks (5)
27 A sailor about to return to make corrections (6)
28 A convenient chap to have around? (8)

Down

1 Tension leading to silver hair (6)
2 An entrance in stone (5)
3 Defeated in protest march and is held for rioting (10)
4 The sticky stuff that could, oddly, grow on... (3)
6 ...grass right by rising river (4)
7 Type of book on marijuana heating unit? (3-6)
8 Relaxed about a heartless football official (8)
10 Doctor to a sporting champion (11)
11 A railway sketch? (4,7)
14 Notice released supporting 9's team (4,6)
15 Chef's position to royal army commander in the past (9)
16 Mix up over 9 with CBS (8)
19 Class that's not so much working (6)

44

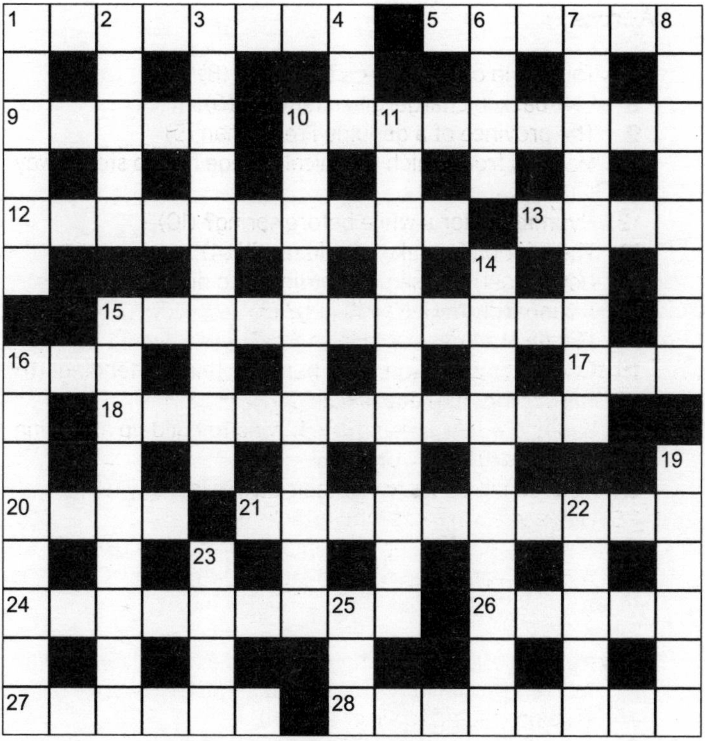

22 Fool changing the ending, in a manner of speaking (5)
23 Lizard point – dangerously wet! (4)
25 A quiet sort of tree? (3)

Across

1 Fight with entrance fees completely waived? (4-3-3)
6 Like style of dress in the south of France (4)
9 Refuse to give incentive to knight (5)
10 Marble's flaw getting golden when covered in tea? (9)
12 When credit is given, it's good to get this piece of paper (4,9)
14 The man wanting new senior women as role models (8)
15 Dilutant in alcoholic drink man knocked back? (6)
17 Choose the French stuff for extra taste on the plate (6)
19 Producer of old newsreels – jerking and woeful (8)
21 Raciest poster that's got naughty dinosaurs! (13)
24 Plant ashes in these places? (9)
25 Some care naturally is needed in combat zone (5)
26 Bean covered over in mayo sauce (4)
27 Tending to stir up trouble in centre with record of events (10)

Down

1 Rubbish engineers initially rejected as safety device (4)
2 Indication of additive in drug that you get woozier after (1-6)
3 March towards the end of this every twelve months (9,4)
4 Make new sort of recording of school chaplain maybe (8)
5 Form of insect right inside rock (5)
7 One church composer offering a mass unpopular with sailors! (7)
8 It's bad, one girl being without English, not being able to read (10)
11 Fling that's not ending? Only a quick romance! (3-5,5)
13 What you find in Chinese restaurants? Meat is gluey! (10)
16 Act that gets a bog seat smashed up, say? (8)
18 My niche could be a sooty sort of place (7)
20 Resets a loose tile (7)

45

22 A quiet boy getting protection at home (5)
23 Wed heartless lass (4)

Across

1 Renewed energy when gale returns (6,4)
6 Cards in a rugby team (4)
8 Upset colonists? (8)
9 State learning in abundance (6)
10 Space for development (8)
11 Last of beef soup (6)
12 Not a profit to be insured against (4)
14 Remarkable communication about a lawyer (7)
18 In a temper go last through arched structure (7)
20 Reportedly puts together the cutter (4)
23 Absolution may be short first (6)
24 No end of malice during exciting jaunt whilst shouting for joy (8)
25 Not fully hearing about organ displacement (6)
26 Grace can't sit out with Yankee (8)
27 Instrument used in Old English outside broadcast first (4)
28 Intricate difficulty with a token of fondness (6-4)

Down

1 Ronald holding up group of soldiers forming cavalry division (8)
2 Actors upsetting revolutionary leader (6)
3 Kind mother (6)
4 Canned like sardines (4-5)
5 Follow 16 to place of disgrace (8)
6 Taking flight (8)
7 Chief one, perhaps (8)
13 Think about when the Spanish copper is included in flood (9)
15 Failing as water is going down (2,3,3)
16 Interview spectators (8)
17 Final shout from barman (4,4)
19 Mats they removed to find gem (8)

46

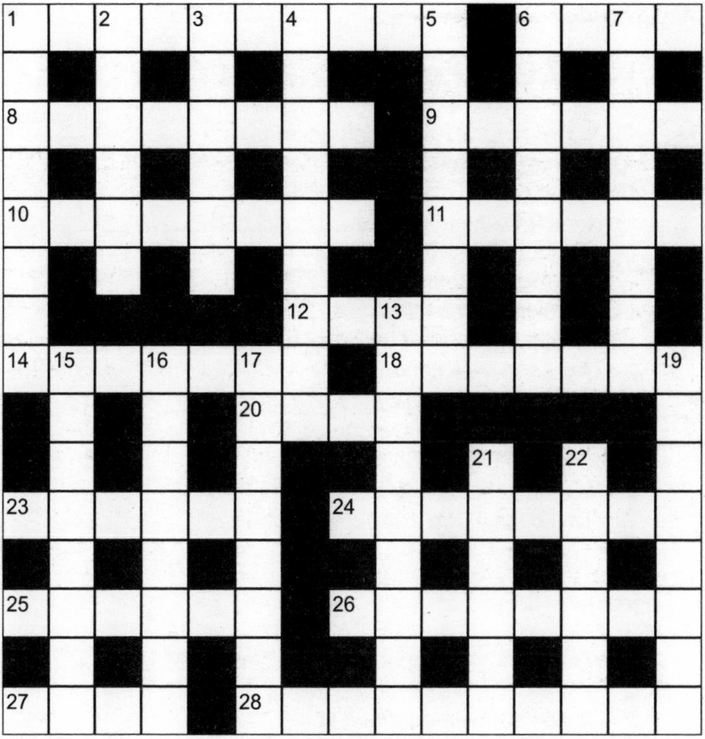

21 Travelling show in Cambridge perhaps (6)
22 Lady creating a minor adjustment (6)

Across

1 Drug user did wrong in law (6)
4 Praised a fantastic garden (8)
9 It's used to lift – or bring down (6)
10 Ship often crossing the bar (8)
12 Bound to have equal scores (4)
13 Restrict king in temporary quarters (5)
14 Church and nest builder (4)
17 Gloomy record playing far on into the night (12)
20 He received his final rents mid-month (6,6)
23 Employer provides a course in the City (4)
24 About in time for match (5)
25 Settled one into residence (4)
28 Someone must have been willing to appoint him (8)
29 A pretty useless object (6)
30 Bandage head with girl's kerchief (8)
31 I'll have a gamble about private accommodation (6)

Down

1 Tied up at work acquiring proficiency (8)
2 A way to serve potatoes, just stuffed with game (8)
3 Inside accommodation (4)
5 Performed with a high degree of skill (12)
6 A cat scrap (4)
7 Region sadly showing neglect (6)
8 Make a mistake and run for it (6)
11 Mayonnaise gets lower rating (8,4)
15 Vehicle holds up progress? Not true (5)
16 Meat skewer, say (5)
18 Sail North, but ordered into port (8)
19 Bank subsidy about to expire (8)
21 Pubs re-built providing choice (6)
22 Humble cleric takes me in (6)
26 Touch up some brass (4)
27 Army team transport (4)

47

Across

1 In the highest position that poet could provide (2,3,3)
5 Refrain from initially challenging mythical deity (6)
9 Unhelpful kind of compassion nobody else can offer (4-4)
10 Aircraft briefly had levelled off (6)
11 Get over insult that's not at all vague (5-3)
12 Inclined to be difficult? (6)
14 Belonging to Tory party? Correct (2,3,5)
18 Trot forward (4-6)
22 Itinerants parking vehicles outside (6)
23 Father backed mother, say – that's obvious (8)
24 Ancient Roman numerals found in theatre (3,3)
25 Left one cat a means of escape (8)
26 Chaps mature as members of household (6)
27 Basically, where this answer goes (2,6)

Down

1 A delicate fabric found around southern part of France (6)
2 Bank worker who produces accounts? (6)
3 Supreme power of politician in Ireland (6)
4 Going beyond striking in pursuit of political position (10)
6 Landing place for some aircraft her pilot arranged (8)
7 Relative standings controlled by monarchy (8)
8 Religious group organised day's toil (8)
13 Kind of turn that could get one into the rep (5-5)
15 Party policy that can raise a person's standing? (8)
16 Switch positions intermittently (3,3,2)
17 Making changes in second part of East End (8)
19 Improvise to produce a note (4,2)
20 Having succeeded, be biased against women (6)
21 Master confused a lot of pupils (6)

48

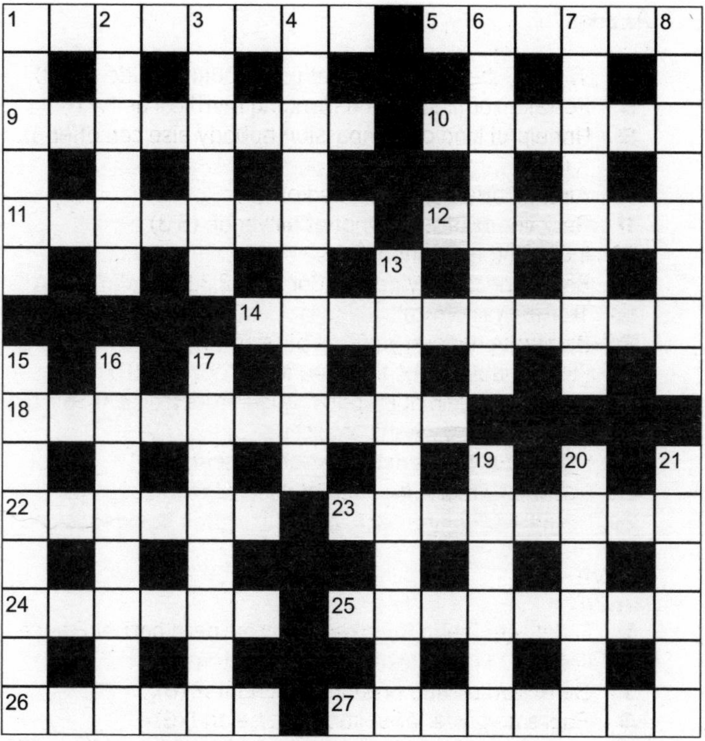

Across

1 Land alternative for this vehicle to work on (7)
9 Go for it in unrestrained fashion (3,5)
10 Motion picture regulated by the cinema scenery... (4,3)
11 ...and theatre ready for expectation of something to come? (5,3)
12 Book concludes the strong feeling of a fanatic (6)
13 According to ranking, hire, we hear, shrewd man (10)
15 Bergamot toilet water produces some essential oil (4)
16 Taint iron chemically by treatment with acid (9)
21 Tranquil midshipman (4)
22 Understanding 'the knowledge' (10)
24 A graduate begins calculus on university's calculator (6)
25 Are kids those who saunter? (8)
27 Smallest dress size mother left behind (7)
28 Soaring right over a fortified location for troops (8)
29 Desmond, looking back, never accepted being ridiculed (7)

Down

2 Realism? Means-test odd clothing items (8)
3 Clone me a breed of lizard (8)
4 Extreme way to leave the trenches (4-3-3)
5 Touched by a material thing (4)
6 Sour beer or a lager perhaps (6)
7 First course, for Stratford players in box office hit, lacks original ingredients (7)
8 Colonize around a place in, say, Washington (7)
11 Even with scores in a mess, obtain the outline plans (9)
14 ET, for instance, has a note on disaffection (10)
17 Deny that over four are not positive (8)
18 Cryptic clues to a meeting of the lips (8)
19 To outshine at the back of the theatre (7)
20 Meddle about with the unrefined manners of Mrs Grundy (7)

49

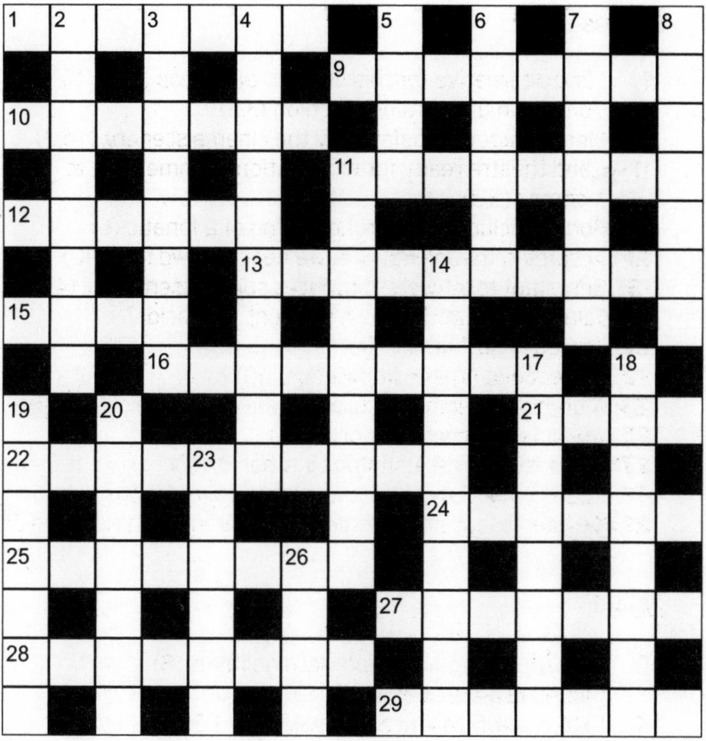

23 Declare some of the French left having eaten one cake (6)
26 Plunder the castle (4)

Across

1 Popular firm and writer making profit (6)
4 Gloria's material to its coverage? (8)
9 Mend poorly instrument broken by number (6)
10 Bishop in Beirut's possibly more stocky (8)
11 Dish around vessel mostly is beef (9)
13 Lock turning in dresser thankfully (5)
14 Notice keen hug misinterpreted ironically (6,2,5)
17 Persuasive discussion by Henry probing obsessive behaviour (6-7)
21 Some ladies' hero in Surrey town (5)
23 A ready source of rags? (9)
24 A dry man disturbed about liberal state (8)
25 Bird without new drink (6)
26 New team not beginning to react? It makes no difference (2,6)
27 A late form of transport? (6)

Down

1 I'm supported by sweetener right away in drink (6)
2 Old artist representing tale in part of poem (9)
3 Asian in US city accommodated by Central American (7)
5 Relative who men trail nervously? (6-2-3)
6 Mechanical crib too unstable (7)
7 Learning to protect single flower (5)
8 Enjoyment following moguls? (5-3)
12 Favour shown by mug (11)
15 Kitchen item, say, by diner consuming good bit of bread (3,6)
16 Archetypal working-class chap taking sun, divorcee, limited by poor means (5,3)
18 Girl permitted small pastry (7)
19 Fancy mailing, not large, spilt at foot of entrance (7)
20 Withhold cheer from staff? About right (6)
22 Rush in front of married women's quarters (5)

50

Across

1 Mum and Dad are in such a state! (10)
9 Be eating the thing making for a light meal (4)
10 Being mesmerised, say something like 'L-E-A-P' (10)
11 Carry on with old lover (nurse) (6)
12 What's greatly disliked – not all escape that, evidently (3,4)
15 Supervise fool when entering wild area (7)
16 Street not allowed to provide ale (5)
17 Garment that's right with a gong? (4)
18 Guess Henry will get the girl (4)
19 Tree that has insect in, by church (5)
21 Explosive theologian given a lift somewhere in Somerset (7)
22 I thump a jerk and act melodramatically (3,2,2)
24 Landowners died in beastly holes (6)
27 Convivial, albeit posh, not straightforward (10)
28 Something in list gone over by site manager (4)
29 General's generous feast (10)

Down

2 A politician's current measures (4)
3 Old implement – it's buried in hole possibly (6)
4 Memorials of those destroyed in battles (7)
5 When we pay for the drinks they are a burden! (4)
6 English rubbish overlooked by accomplished French philosopher (7)
7 Minor road that could wind round to desert site (4,6)
8 New helper said to show ability to take initiative (10)
12 Keep behind this gate? (10)
13 In stable we poured out drinks (5,5)
14 Number three in wrong sequence (5)
15 Artist is champ (5)
19 Poor entertainment not at all well done! (3,4)

51

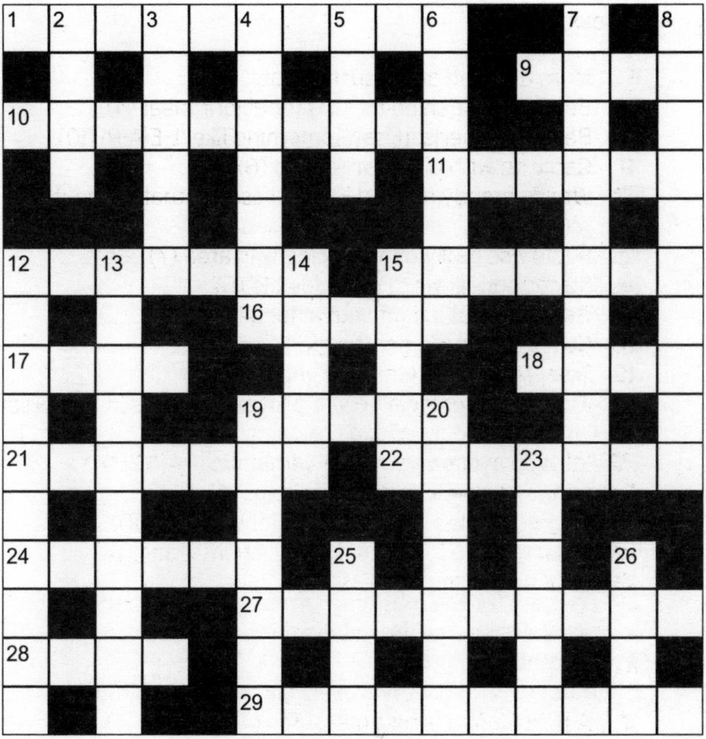

20 They stop tiles coming loose (7)
23 I am two and get spoilt (6)
25 Employed in house, dusting (4)
26 Writer was ill, endlessly upset (4)

Across

1 Steps up the retreat (6)
9 Is in Palestine or off the coast of Northumberland (4,6)
10 Charitable event noble arranged (10)
11 Bird, one ousted by young lover (4)
12 The shopping area in London? (4)
14 Be instructed to become ordained (4,6)
17 In an advantageous position with money inside (5,2)
18 Practising the art of eating out (7)
20 Step not made by one going forwards (10)
21 Whitish stake (4)
22 51 in company of Muse (4)
23 Motorists' preserve? (7,3)
25 One of the field parking has splendid hat (4-6)
26 Fellow drawing back to get sacred text (6)

Down

2 Learned for the most part on river printed matter (10)
3 Stare at extreme characters for example turning out (4)
4 Breathtaking (10)
5 Purely theoretical, it is over our heads on sunny days (4-3)
6 Droop with immediate loss thus initially (4)
7 Union restriction less often seen nowadays on a Sunday (6,4)
8 Fuss over Northern Ireland's handsome youth (6)
13 Having gone first, Ernest had stockings inside leather shorts (10)
15 Do better than someone else emerging from troupe (10)
16 Instigator troubled grenadier travelling round lake (10)
19 Tool piercing board is subject to duty (7)
20 I creep over to produce formula (6)
23 Sound horn up and down (4)
24 Firm in the money (4)

52

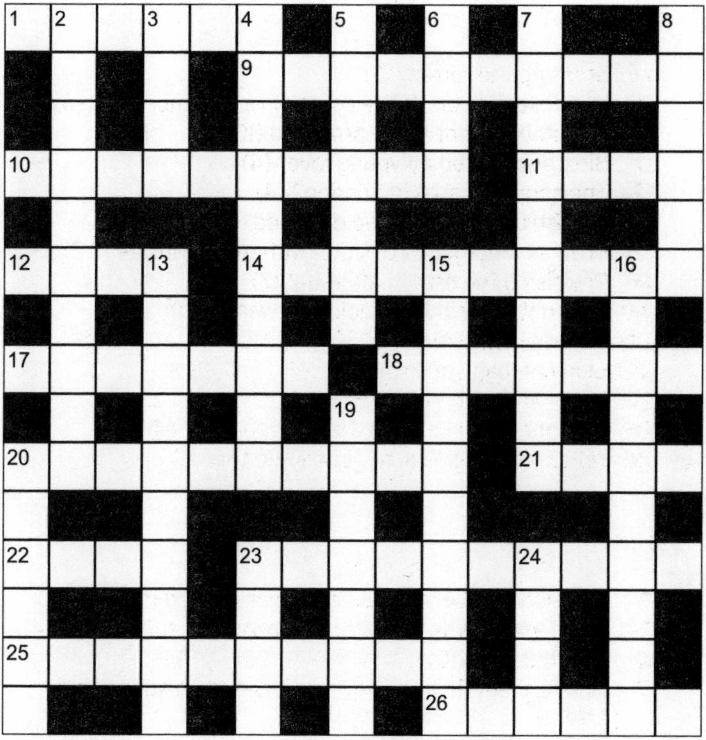

Across

7 Fire and unload (9)
8 Simple soul was penniless (5)
10 Pressing need for home club (8)
11 Acted evasively, being naturally guarded (6)
12 Bird-talk (4)
13 Broken leg is set by linesmen (8)
15 Why answer? (7)
17 Conceal that the cost of insurance has risen? (5,2)
20 Club regulation that must be strictly obeyed (4,4)
22 It may accompany the drum in eastern Scotland (4)
25 A pop song creature (6)
26 A machine to tune with skill (8)
27 Money advanced for empty apartment (5)
28 Plan game anew after false start (9)

Down

1 Admit defeat and return (5)
2 Put down a whisky (6)
3 Gives information which could lead to making an arrest (8)
4 In age so twisted, suffering pains (7)
5 Inaccurate shooting, but it can spread destruction (8)
6 Crucial to take doctor and soldiers to America (9)
9 Female with hole in her footwear (4)
14 Pot of ale? (4,5)
16 Bill accepts name is incorrect, his memory is at fault (8)
18 A cricketer's sick leave? (3-5)
19 For which a damp course is essential (7)
21 Yet such a description may be fair comment (4)
23 A learner joins class that's strict (6)
24 Remove top from box to reveal present (5)

53

Across

1 Cheerful at college buffet (6)
4 Crown duke media exploited (6)
8 A card game daughter cut short (8)
10 Colour of boy's terrier (6)
11 Man with hock (4)
12 Shriek catching a boy dressing (5,5)
13 Polite, Pickwick's servant bringing in German writer and editor (4-8)
16 Lots go here after prices tumble? (5,7)
20 Always a great moment accompanying head of state (2,3,5)
21 Name wood after famous town planner (4)
22 Cowardly, cat initially facing Poe's talking bird! (6)
23 Plant fake diamond (8)
24 One of unquestioning obedience with unknown means abroad (3-3)
25 Struggle in variety (6)

Down

1 Left bishop inside, not out (8)
2 Child, one entering farm building (5)
3 Imposing, a state capital (7)
5 OK neat? (2,5)
6 Record by embarrassed Italian causes harm to reputation (9)
7 Dame, an inebriated bacchante (6)
9 US songwriter, disciple of Welsh poet (5,6)
14 The Parisienne upset Yves' old flames (4-5)
15 Icon's car damaged coming from Ajaccio? (8)
17 Short film associated with a fairy queen (7)
18 Arrogant type on horseback, last to cross cutting (7)
19 Factory ultimately supporting shop floor (6)
21 Operatic work, not quite typical (5)

54

Across

1 Growing ability to provide amounts of Chartreuse? (5,7)
8 Opening in theatre school (7)
9 Cunning is needed in any breakdown of law and order (7)
11 Title is arranged for a select few (7)
12 Cricket side before test being judged (2,5)
13 Connection with cup match at home (3-2)
14 Unusually neat prose nobody speaks, naturally (9)
16 Frequent need for drinking of sailors from Irish port (9)
19 A kind of European partner (5)
21 Initial situations in office where posts are distributed (2-5)
23 Pragmatic view is taken in kingdom (7)
24 Irritating arrangement of bars (7)
25 A pair of card-players with amount of money said to be incredible (7)
26 Memorable occasion as character's trapped by snake turning nasty, finally (3-6,3)

Down

1 Christian, for example, is kind, sheltering one (7)
2 Rebellious activity lacking leader – that's an issue (7)
3 In the raw, sadly, without good evening dress? (9)
4 I had a house in this state (5)
5 King following dishonest operator (7)
6 I see you are, so to speak, not involved in this disturbance (7)
7 Intellectual female conveying sadness to cold ruler (12)
10 Wild bird or chicken hit really hard (12)
15 Political supporters of soldier imprisoned by monarch lacking virtue (5,4)
17 Artist gets only a little in ruthless competition (3,4)
18 Salesman's glib talk takes in an obsequious type (7)
19 Impasse reached by many of the characters in Hamlet (4,3)

55

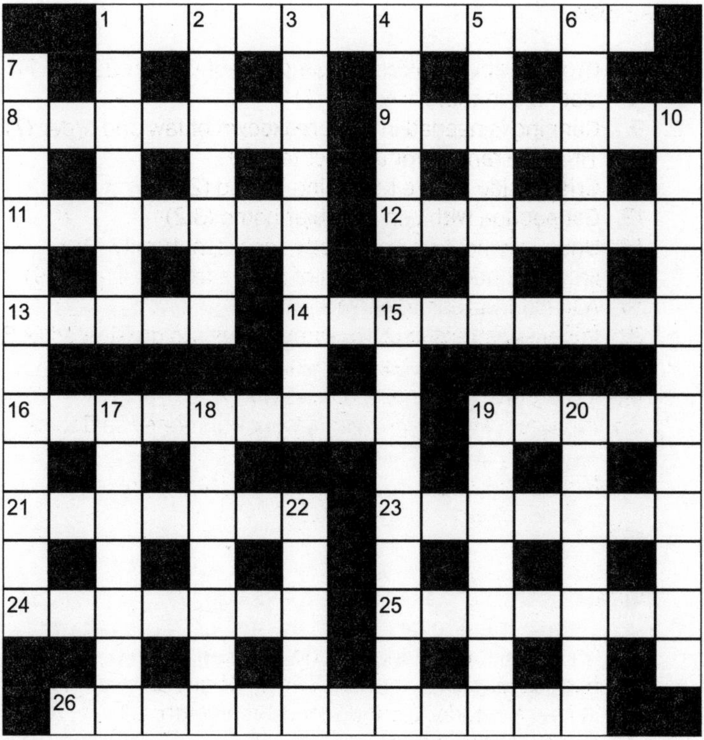

20 I keep records in attempt to produce series of books (7)
22 Aid for marksman, in a sense (5)

Across

1 Traditional gift - open with anger! (12)
9 Men are kids! (4)
10 Unconventional rice dish containing American c-coin (9)
12 Look for respect (6)
13 Modern day ballot accepting accountant and lawyer (8)
15 The genius behind smart denim dress? (10)
16 When reversing it makes wine (4)
18 Ride a white horse (4)
20 In a ski run a disaster for these nationals (10)
23 Become edgy during trade payment (8)
24 Boxes with energy, being thin (6)
26 Colleague fighting seats welcomes no agents (9)
27 A round of applause for the worker (4)
28 Germany is almost illegal - note the difference! (12)

Down

2 Diffident, but half of rent was enough (8)
3 Requirement to be born on the first of December (4)
4 Casual and popular detectives with endless talent displayed (10)
5 France's refusal to support prison arm (6)
6 French people with no right to crew on Sunday (7)
7 Lancashire town ties as set out in this book (12)
8 Another book, but for magistrates (6)
11 The perfect place for intended touchdown? (8,4)
14 Warning given before the great fire of London? (5,5)
17 Crack marksman gets exposure (8)
19 Denies soldiers the means to set off explosives (7)
21 A right harangue - and thorough! (6)
22 Free car use given to cupholder (6)
25 List that's a bit thin on the ground (4)

56

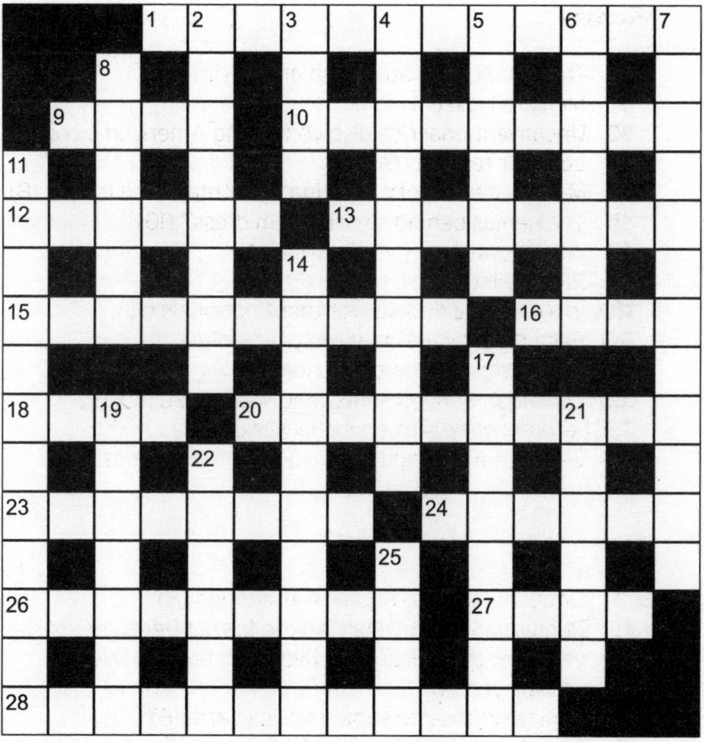

Across

8 Mum, getting terribly hot, ran in race (8)
9 Living things and landscape man found by river (6)
10 Precipitation said to be expected (3)
11 Jumpers needed for this playground activity (8)
12 Fuss when gull goes round field (6)
13 Tired men ruined one country, being unable to make decisions (15)
15 Beastly ten-legged combination that brings fear (7)
18 Loose American gang round the end of town (7)
21 Match of contrasts made up by Georgia and me! (4,2,3,6)
24 Trip into lands afar indescribable (6)
25 Notes are struck to evoke memories, maybe (8)
26 Become weak with endless cycle of duty (3)
27 Get rid of hindrance blocking river (6)
28 Go in halo to sort out ruffian (8)

Down

1 Collapse with cold when having a streak! (4,2)
2 Daughter given fruit that's splotchy (6)
3 Hear Cardiff sage, unusually diplomatic sort of chap (6,1'8)
4 It suggests that mate may be approaching (7)
5 Six-legged combination of best friends doing a job at 12? (3,3,3,3,3)
6 Expanse of water where you could see flying tit – canal? (8)
7 Oil beginning to exude under wrecked scooter (8)
14 Appreciate deprecatory comment (3)
16 Girl's going round Herts town unexpectedly (8)
17 Yeoman of the guard releasing female bird (3-5)
19 Maybe the curate's noisy action on bike (3)
20 Bashful about skin lump that's blackish (7)
22 To some extent corpulent, I love a bit of food (6)
23 Catch parent out (6)

57

Across

1 Observe missile entering plant (6)
4 Closely follow notice in exhibition (6)
8 Cousin travelling round Bahamas at a relatively great speed (8)
10 A worry erupted about missiles (6)
11 Strain first Italian vehicle (4)
12 Unit go on horseback in front of trail left by animals that is colourful! (10)
13 Eminent composer? (6,2,4)
16 Anona had sauce with fruit (7-5)
20 Way of thinking where station may be found on radio (10)
21 Dull eastern tea! (4)
22 More adroit without Kay using bread-knife (6)
23 Win easily coming from playhouse! (4,4)
24 Lady rejecting a novel alternative (6)
25 Some boys' term for marine creature (6)

Down

1 Piglet perhaps or rat (8)
2 Dish, huss I cooked (5)
3 Brief reference, say (7)
5 Stop at sea (5,2)
6 Price of shop-soiled goods? (4-5)
7 Amazing ordinary women in the side (6)
9 Highly suspenseful story of rock-climber? (11)
14 One exempt from criticism found on Indian street (6,3)
15 Grandfather clock (3-5)
17 Retains reconstituted fatty part (7)
18 Old country lady went round Head Office initially before end of day (7)
19 Turnkey mixed oil inside pot (6)
21 Surprised exclamation about first person's headgear (2,3)

58

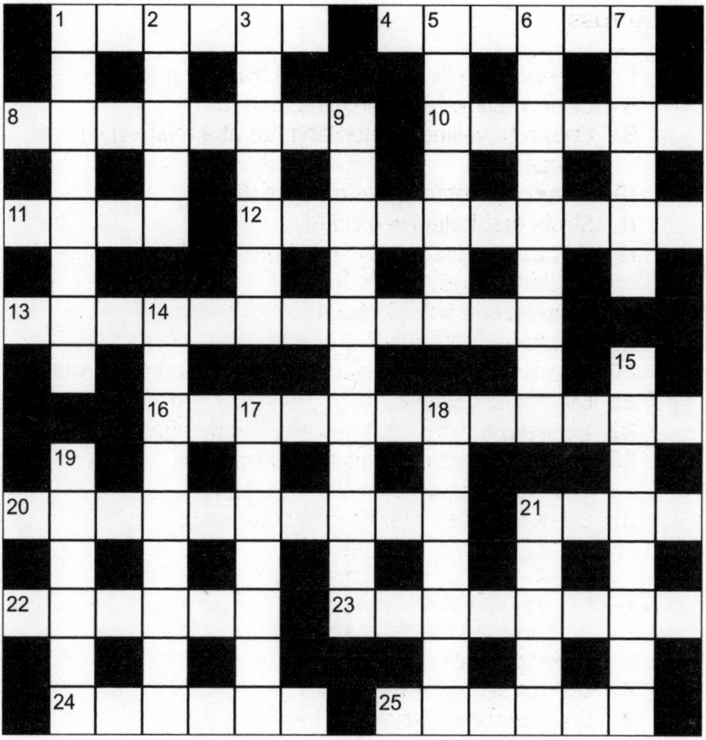

Across

1 Man uses mashie and spoon going round (4,7)
9 Current increase in rent, rising again (9)
10 Affair of one such as Othello, say (5)
11 Brilliant discovery announced by Archimedes (6)
12 When a girl may scream in case of necessity (2,1,5)
13 Fights for left-overs (6)
15 Left for dead (8)
18 One never knows what it may hold for the present (5,3)
19 Comes down with something for the cat (6)
21 Legal actions taken by a holiday-maker (8)
23 Liberty, for example, is not just a figure of speech (6)
26 Work-time entertainment (5)
27 Annoyed girl, having tried awkwardly to embrace her (9)
28 Cash offer you can't refuse (5,6)

Down

1 Fit to work like a horse (7)
2 He keeps far too much to himself (5)
3 Dissatisfied workers will be out to get it (6,3)
4 Take off a ring, we hear (4)
5 Championship secured in final with style (8)
6 Fly biting (5)
7 Protected from shock, but still broken-hearted (7)
8 To surpass score is excellent (3-5)
14 Criminal who runs a bankrupt business (8)
16 A great thinker, tries a lot to be different (9)
17 Rise drunkenly to get Heather some wine (8)
18 Be open-handed or use one's fists? (4,3)
20 No mean poet! (7)
22 Swim before one can walk (5)
24 Carried, to a man (5)
25 With regular absences, four fail exam (4)

59

Across

1 More dreadful endless trendy church service (7)
9 Immoral act ended in stir? (8)
10 Go off and set about heartless fairy (7)
11 Head of state going on but trailing (8)
12 Condescend to include Scottish leader in representation (6)
13 Imperfect MP I elect, no change (10)
15 Current compiler's high point (4)
16 Breakdown out in Iran, possibly (9)
21 Flat race isn't finished (4)
22 Teaches it's changing appreciation of beauty (10)
24 Tory ends holding advanced score (6)
25 Stalwart of Pop Art is Andy... (8)
27 Hide from sweetheart in panic (7)
28 Conceals mysteries around end of code (8)
29 Pardon girl taking refuge (7)

Down

2 Luxury of clue with open resolution... (8)
3 ...the answer's a riddle! (8)
4 To sleep, perchance to dream? (10)
5 Producer of sugar cane, say (4)
6 Turn vote before a grand race (6)
7 Established act constraining police (7)
8 Good actor's ringing pitch (7)
11 Bigoted, as certain could be (9)
14 Normal guy's taking one side, embracing right (10)
17 Write article on new Ecstasy drug (8)
18 Most cross river gripping chains (8)
19 Prickly pine hides snake (7)
20 Bird's after big time lush (7)
23 Came down hard on everyone? (6)
26 Last word from alpha males (4)

60

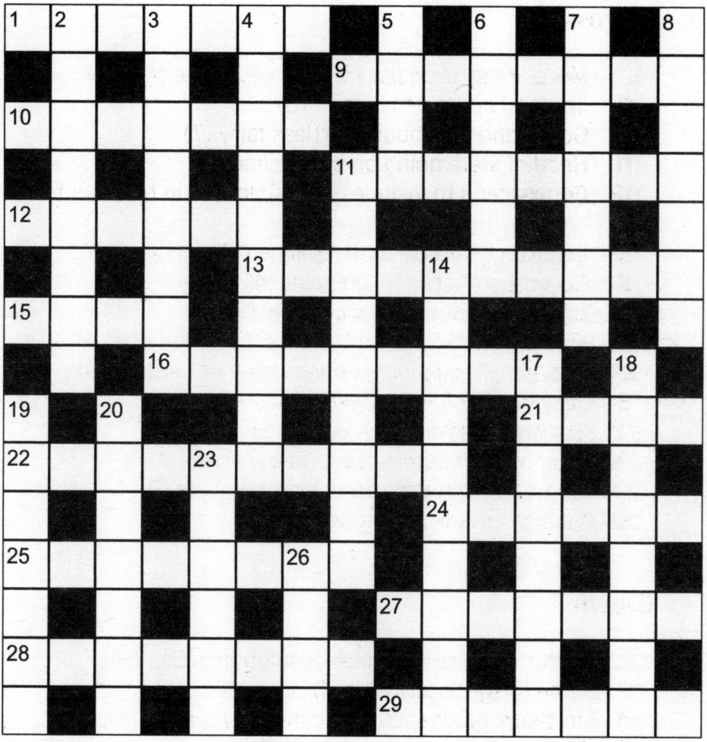

Across

1 Official statement to crowd about tenancy agreement (5,7)
9 Fielder's mistake (4)
10 One excluded strange island abroad (3,3,3)
12 Irritable old servants (6)
13 Taste our fresh fish (3,5)
15 Lampstands precariously balanced by artist (10)
16 Landmass – between seas, I assume (4)
18 Band from the south has reformed (4)
20 Monument – one layer within gets treated (10)
23 Mexican with stock managed company employing that woman (8)
24 Fear brawl must involve leader of rabble (6)
26 Gone out with one cutting art gallery deal (9)
27 Keen, prima donna? On the contrary (4)
28 Publican in car next to curator (6-6)

Down

2 Banter concerning role, extremely emotive (8)
3 Demonstration succeeded – and how! (4)
4 Misleading clue embarrassed Holmes, initially slipping up (3,7)
5 Slowly encircling a shed (4-2)
6 Passionate – that could be us after a second run out (7)
7 English country gentlemen holding answer for realtors (6,6)
8 Time for morning coffee in the Spanish square? (6)
11 Girl's coming across bound for a place down under (5,7)
14 Talk much about little sailor, a toad (10)
17 A dearth? Gather so, surprisingly (8)
19 Country girl seen weaving ahead (7)
21 Drink in a mug (6)
22 Got the shakes in run-down part of city (6)
25 Lake in Maine, centre for crew (4)

61

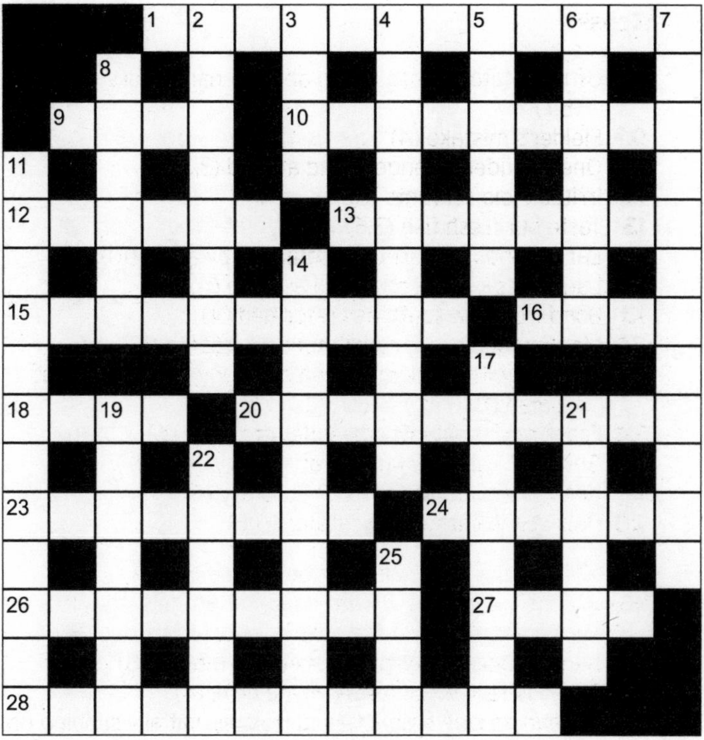

Across

8 English book containing good summary (7)
10 Rolling work curtailed fast (7)
11 Close fitting? Good when in this knit woolly (9)
12 March trailed by new energetic figure (5)
13 Recurrent idea from article by writer (5)
14 Maritime event having at sea great set of volunteers (7)
17 Unexciting location dividing traffic? (6-2-3-4)
19 Fans for rioting in orange (7)
21 Relative close to café in French place (5)
24 Reportedly, modify part of church (5)
26 Imaginary spillage of oil in fact (9)
27 Priest accepting a nuclear facility (7)
28 Titled woman of the French game (7)

Down

1 Black plant for wealthy globetrotters? (3,3)
2 Bonus having girl, 6, with daughter around study? (8)
3 Brutish chap we let tiro stupidly start to respect (10)
4 Noted Croat sadly stripped of new academic honour (9)
5 Cheesy stuff from Asian, we hear (4)
6 Ambassador left satisfied gaining capital protection (6)
7 Conventional rallying point (8)
9 BBC official in middle of week gets advantage (4)
15 Part of course by fellow in Switzerland for flighty creature (10)
16 She departed in incendiary circumstances (4,2,3)
17 A mess with car crashing – and carnage! (8)
18 Bloomer made by old Greek hero (8)
20 Overpaid executive given some grief at cathedral (3,3)
22 Recruit bridge players with catalogue (6)
23 Gust caused by missile? (4)
25 Learner swapping halves in sandwich (4)

62

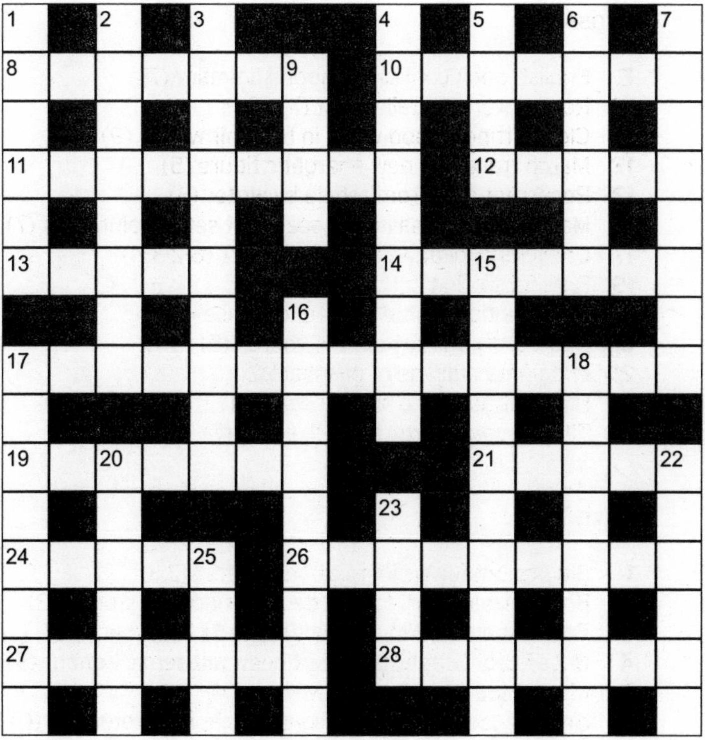

Across

7 Urbane MP in new deal that's a bit shady (8)
9 Hot number getting top position perhaps (6)
10 Say, member is drowning in beer! (6)
11 Drip is getting worse and it brings dismay (8)
12 Never stopping as revolutions go on (6-3-5)
15 Wartime food plans put back (4)
17 Car goes on wheels (5)
19 Dairy product manufactured the wrong way (4)
20 Birthday bonus that's nice but superficial? (5,2,3,4)
23 Heather invading weakens young trees (8)
25 Light-heartedness of priest starts to trouble you (6)
27 Girl somersaulting in gym reveals feathery things (6)
28 Like language from fellow turning hysterical (8)

Down

1 Big Ben? Made a big noise, not half! (4)
2 Boyfriend appearing outside old city office (6)
3 Poet not allowed in the auditorium (4)
4 Characters with atrophy, sickness getting rare old medicine (6)
5 Organic compound that can be made from nice oils (8)
6 Psychiatrist here again? Cringe (6,4)
8 Kitchen item available from book library maybe! (7)
13 Agent with strange dialect gets copied (10)
14 Beautiful female as captured by the lens (5)
16 The most important course? Mum's in agreement (4,4)
18 Pupil going off in car – hols! (7)
21 River foremen abandoning river (6)
22 Warning when tiger's seen round the road? (6)
24 Wise man not finishing a long account (4)
26 The border he cut is neat (4)

63

Across

7 Dull fellows of the cloth are unseen establishment figures (3,2,4,5)
9 Stinging complaint? (6-4)
11 Set about including a surfeit (4)
12 A couple of pounds, that's as many as there are (3)
13 Disconcerting procrastination (3-7)
16 In Brazil, expected to find Holly (4)
17 Stepwise arrangement of hierarchy? (7)
18 Amphibian pecked aquatic plant (7)
20 Tailless animal in portico (4)
21 Draw tail, result disastrous (10)
23 One does not approve when this is repeated (3)
24 No time is lost at this (4)
25 Desk, one found in dilapidated rectories (10)
28 Formal protest about gift (14)

Down

1 Not quite right to speak in it? (9,5)
2 One in France, it is one (4)
3 Joint bent in submission (4)
4 Interrupt illegal act (5-2)
5 Gosh, a party was thrown for old mathematician (10)
6 Muckraker makes something dirty last for a long time (10)
8 Until the beer runs out? (2,3,6,3)
10 Odd characters look up at diminutive lady! (3)
14 Awkward red-tape ie right to be included for secondary lodging (4-1-5)
15 Relaxed, what shoplifter did was not difficult, some might say (4,2,4)
19 Putting in the first three (7)
22 Make lace using inferior articles (3)
26 Terrorists question the country (4)
27 Roman poet did nothing with six old pence (4)

64

Across

1 Become a success and travel (2,6)
6 Customs that suit many riders (6)
9 Transport for student with a university final (6)
10 Rare lily found broken in the chaff (8)
11 American Indian organisation of coachmen (8)
12 Meal causes quarrel at home (6)
13 A butchery firm owned by a combine? (5,7)
16 Upset when given an open transfer? (7,5)
19 Arm one in a club (6)
21 They open out for the novice (8)
23 Powerful passage of literature? (8)
24 A plant Sam has to look out for (6)
25 A problem? He's only kidding (6)
26 A blow for the farmworker (8)

Down

2 He gives people his address (6)
3 Girl in scholarly dialogue (5)
4 Famous statesman badly led by the clergy (9)
5 Old instrument of temptation (7)
6 Give a lift to one in the army (5)
7 Impudent type? (4-5)
8 Rows about stray dogs (8)
13 They have time to finish (9)
14 Lou and Ivy sob together, uncontrollably and openly (9)
15 Novel is remote and tedious (8)
17 Not a subject put on in advance (7)
18 Snooker on the green? (6)
20 Added recommendation for a jockey (5)
22 Party-giver is given a plant (5)

65

Across

6 Policeman putting criminals before bench (9)
7 Establish there's nothing in kitty (5)
10 Ditches yobs embracing right (7)
11 Useless scrap by rotten drunk (6)
12 Let rip? (4)
13 Application of tax includes queen (8)
15 Drool with yen for bondage (7)
17 Rubble contains little for popular stone (7)
20 A censor changed about one script (8)
22 Chronic fatigue containing Iran's mess (4)
25 America's head considered distracted (6)
26 From internet, ran site for travel (7)
27 Intelligent? No, and not erudite initially (5)
28 Common mayor cuts transport (9)

Down

1 Kick start hard after stall (5)
2 Having debarked tree with raw material (6)
3 Left following sound of hilarity (8)
4 Labour leader in famous general assembly (7)
5 Tortured genius had trouble (9)
8 Lawman using force if assaulted (7)
9 Cocaine's about acceptable before Ecstasy (4)
14 The French stick by party leader's job (9)
16 Meat cooked in ovens? (7)
18 Condemn a good man in blame shifting (8)
19 After radio ends, play guitar on stage (7)
21 Sudden regret engulfs daughter (4)
23 Recover from breakdown? (6)
24 Heart of Essex bird is cruel (5)

66

Across

7 Just send a message to Commonwealth general (7)
8 Alarm about article hidden in eiderdown (7)
10 Control law-enforcement groups going to Jerusalem (10)
11 It's a driver's warning, anyway (4)
12 Scholarly and admirably recited (4-4)
14 It's derisory to put press in charge (6)
15 Take the blame before transfer to prison (5,3,3)
19 Her Parisian husband is getting on (6)
20 Groom's work is preparing Indian stew (8)
22 Market speculator brings back guns (4)
23 Flog this to get theatrical aids (10)
25 Performer embraces comic widow (7)
26 Expert takes a look at wild ox (7)

Down

1 His cart vanished during the conflict (7)
2 Arm French cupholders (4)
3 Indian religionist of equal value to diocese (6)
4 Aim to get schedule in the interval (8)
5 Still providing office materials, they say (10)
6 Lay down slices of topside (7)
9 It puts veracity to the test (3,8)
13 Star heading to offshore isle (7,3)
16 No tears from tenants living thus! (4-4)
17 Fellow takes steps to unearth dissentious group (7)
18 This month everything gets put in place (7)
21 Arrive with a cheap cigarette (4,2)
24 Soldier given paper as a handout (4)

67

Across

1 Problem when running a streaker never has (6)
5 Irritates son - that's uncalled-for (8)
9 Adjusted his target to right, more perpendicular (10)
10 British island attached to a part of US (4)
11 Rum galore is found in sultan's palace (8)
12 Responsibility of carrier, perhaps (6)
13 Putting silver on tin could produce problem (4)
15 Scary type with an inclination to conceal weapon (8)
18 Damage in fraudulent operation is causing pain (8)
19 Travel document is required to enter Eastern state (4)
21 Admiral in the hold (6)
23 Measure of intelligence at university, breaking silly rules to get drinks (8)
25 It erupted disastrously in Vietnam (4)
26 Finished with part of play, I have become too busy (10)
27 Descent or ascent arranged by railway (8)
28 Fish in Billingsgate going astray (6)

Down

2 Article about it providing support for church (5)
3 & 20 London home of 12 that's under 21 and in front of 5D (9,6)
4 As we hear, witch will bargain (6)
5 State-of-the-art building? Just the opposite! (8,7)
6 Are one up, possibly, like half the players in Ryder Cup (8)
7 Being dishonent, having position that's not upright (5)
8 Noticed stable support for working with timber (9)
14 One of the last men in top political position (6,3)
16 Celebrity doctor struggles with problem for smokers (5,4)
17 Add name and publish travel guide (8)
20 See 3
22 Condition of New York or Washington, say (5)
24 Behead chicken or another bird (5)

68

Across

1 This person, 50, outwardly shy, good-looking (6)
4 Brief stay in hotel? That must be pots! (8)
9 Accepting a ruler after short time (6)
10 Framework that's minimal, somehow not sleek (8)
11 One hoping for a catch in the deep? (9)
13 The unending quarrel produced by project (5)
14 Rave-up devoid of drugs? This person may have been wronged (8,5)
17 Tyrannical writer meets Italian heretic (13)
21 Plunge into water from window senselessly (5)
23 Daring USA duo involved with CIA (9)
24 Breed of cattle torn apart by the lions (8)
25 Herb may be entertained by women divers (6)
26 Put off job, one involving little power (8)
27 Moderate slope skier initially missed (6)

Down

1 Strike outside to end (3,3)
2 Temporary force - workers over the night period? (9)
3 Departed around start of night with sailors following light (7)
5 Deceived worker could be so looked after... (5,2,4)
6 ...as could be this computer (7)
7 One making choice against old books with little hesitation (5)
8 Fugitives manage when crossing path (8)
12 Plot to achieve speed of sound at start of race (11)
15 Jumble in dream so puzzling (9)
16 Parish had somehow to avoid a disaster (8)
18 Dance that was a significant thing for first man on moon (3-4)
19 Something that may be burning in awful scene (7)

69

20 State a thing that's sure to be heard (6)
22 City's water supplies (5)

Across

3 Covered as a safeguard (2,4)
6 Piece of sugar with a root? (4)
8 Sailor goes to the edge completely full (5)
9 Small animal before train was used for postal delivery (4,7)
10 Fake sweetmeat (5)
11 Reversing after day at work perhaps? (7,4)
16 Made time inside for continental lady (6)
17 Holding back the satin design (8)
19 One lady in Greek character's clutches, new Welsh lady (8)
20 Commander found tailless rodents reproducing without fertilisation! (6)
22 Obvious case (4-3-4)
25 One getting up vertical pipe (5)
27 With increasing speed on the piano perhaps (11)
28 Without stopping very much (2,3)
29 Feeling of resentment when messenger loses ring (4)
30 Let the bathwater out? (6)

Down

1 Herein a local farm animal (4)
2 Crossing approach road to reach tournament (6-5)
3 Encumbrances one with defect preventing free speech first (11)
4 Frank may have performed (6)
5 Sample different spice, fellows (8)
6 About to carry off chocolate substitute (5)
7 Primary scholar, one entering Signal Corps (5)
12 Leaving using force doing well (5,6)
13 Dread plan for deterring burglars (5,6)
14 Inferior work of art from Christopher's companion (6)
15 Reorganised more by first stage (6)
18 Central American hound ran round (8)

70

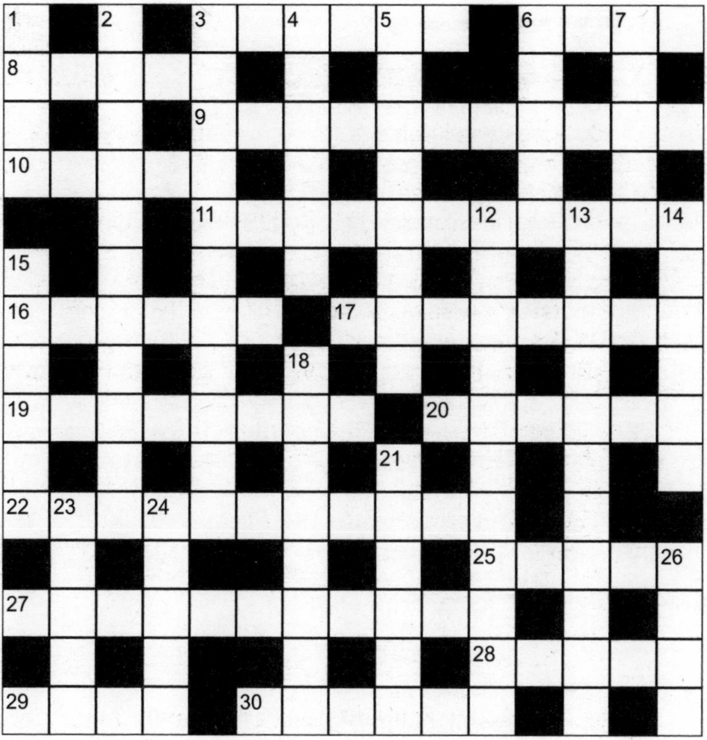

21 Help one endlessly dispersing disinfectant (6)
23 Nut has power training first (5)
24 Poor marshal accepted limited edition (5)
26 Rugby theologian had fish (4)

Across

1 Cash reserves (6)
4 A barrier to progress for some races (8)
9 Is in a hide to see a bird (6)
10 We take a call about silver speculation (8)
12 Terrible ruler of vain disposition (4)
13 After time, ceremony becomes commonplace (5)
14 The Spanish doctor – a saint to sailors (4)
17 The pals adore variety, though difficult to satisfy (4,2,6)
20 Beginner's course in French (4,1'7)
23 Workers' home (4)
24 Intends to make money (5)
25 Keen to help a number inside (4)
28 Figure of importance in American defence (8)
29 One takes no end of cash in here, finishing with nothing (6)
30 Aggravates school-head? That's not called for (8)
31 Dislike writing notes before exam (6)

Down

1 Eat chips in a way that's not original (8)
2 Where you might finish if you take flight (8)
3 Welshman's making a stand (4)
5 Get up before ten (4,3,5)
6 Restrictions imposed for cup matches (4)
7 It's hot to the tongue, cold to the ear (6)
8 Urges preparation for breakfast? (4,2)
11 Stop our peers' recreation? Outrageous! (12)
15 Get down to dividing bribe (5)
16 Publication for children (5)
18 It makes perfect doctors (8)
19 Suited to change, knowing what it's like (4,2,2)
21 Composer writes feature about musical work (6)
22 A meeting-place in the suburban street? (6)

71

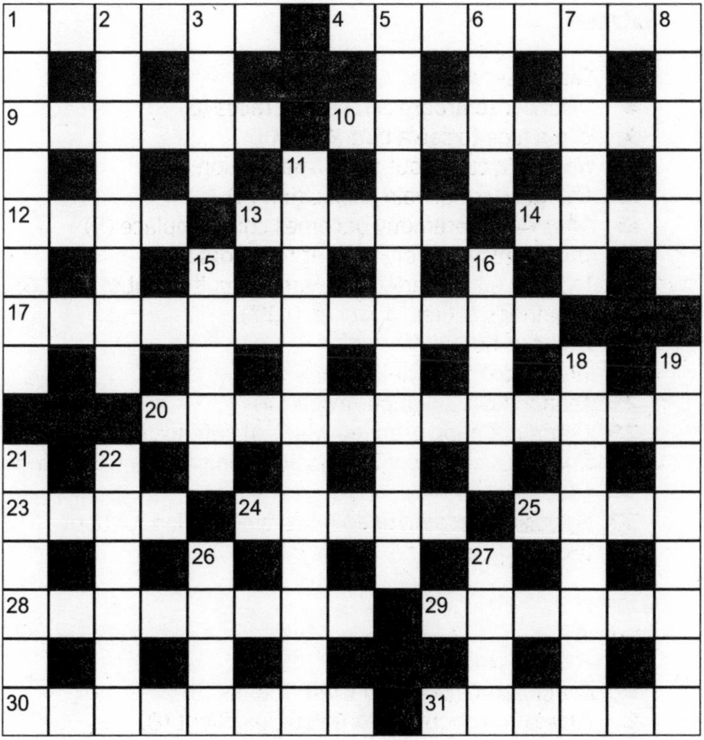

26 Shout and dance, say (4)
27 Found to be contemptible (4)

Across

1 Impress producing great port (8)
5 Flipping fabulous bird put on girdle (6)
9 Brewing ale and demon drink (8)
10 Fish needing both hands in sea (6)
12 Poison remedy around tip of arrow, right? (6)
13 Stony route with bad bends (8)
15 Save other half (7)
16 Report of food hand out (4)
20 Policemen trailing a tart (4)
21 Stops putting expenses on account (7)
25 Preparation for Tory leader in power, say (8)
26 It provides blanket coverage (6)
28 Composer's hit, gripping work (6)
29 Poor on crime, do change English leader (8)
30 Dull service for the audience (6)
31 Appoint European member in time (8)

Down

1 Relief from Sun and Star? (6)
2 Daughter in a jam? Fancy (6)
3 Liberal, one urges reform (8)
4 Man sounds useful (4)
6 From bishop, a question's unclear (6)
7 Worried, admitting left recovered (8)
8 More caring, he proposes (8)
11 Ace group playing dump (7)
14 Dirty old boy in front of stage (7)
17 Broadcast a lunatic marine (8)
18 Having too many troubles in Eastenders? (8)
19 Drug, on a trip, smashed on Ecstasy (8)
22 Absolute fury by hospital department (6)
23 Bush, perhaps, angry initially about secret service (6)

72

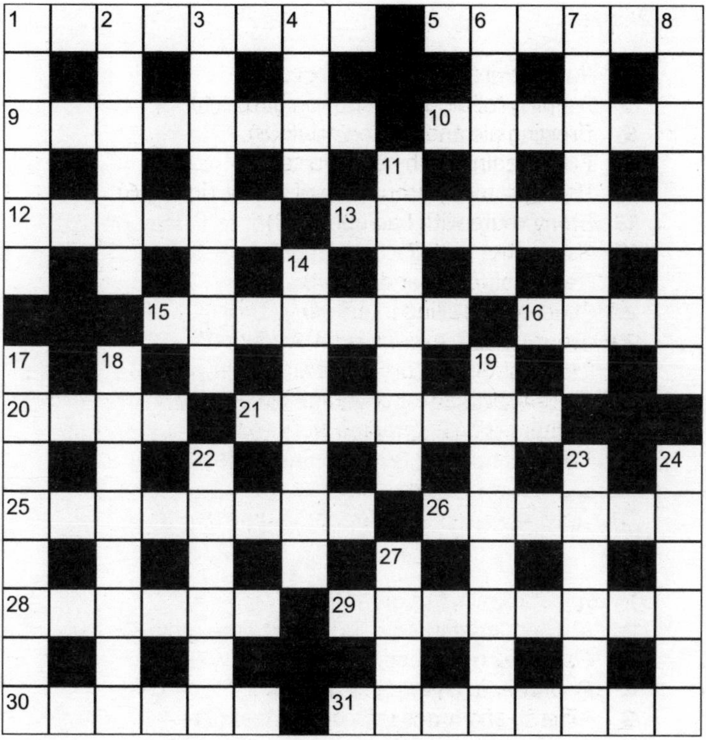

24 Present company previously getting stick (6)
27 Fair time in charge (4)

Across

7 Hound Marxist problemist (3,6)
8 N. European captured Irish leading lady (5)
10 Lengthy complaint made awful maid jeer (8)
11 Patriotic song puts worker on edge (6)
12 Some militant, indigenous terrorists are hostile (4)
13 Oriental fighter-plane gathers speed to leave land (8)
15 Philosopher goes round America in a banger (7)
17 Conference engenders tedious fuss (7)
20 Church with a forthright minister (8)
22 Given credit for exposing parasite (4)
25 It's not so hot in the slammer (6)
26 Andy and girl scrambled in audacious style (8)
27 Distinguished elderly relative died (5)
28 Fastness housing British dignitary (9)

Down

1 Fellow always has great anxiety (5)
2 A strict understanding to keep to the rear (6)
3 Conspicuous way to hit the economy (8)
4 Receiver used by top stream (7)
5 Plant in which waiter is maltreated (8)
6 Uneasy after peacekeepers made deal (9)
9 One Socialist returned from paradise island (4)
14 Rush by committee to produce instrument panel (9)
16 Oust petitioner when I leave (8)
18 No treaty is arranged without him (8)
19 I noted a change when counting calories (2,1,4)
21 A gipsy gentleman utterly out of order (4)
23 Eccentric accepts an ill-founded rumour (6)
24 Many reluctant to take the stuff (5)

73

Across

1 Went over to jazz incorporating jingle (9)
6 Precise demand (5)
9 Pins ribs (7)
10 Temple too rundown to be a tribal symbol (5-4)
11 More elaborate cooking's not rare (7)
12 We hear that North hill-range is found in East Anglia (7)
13 Mutual trust in the midst of helplessness (15)
18 Let's eat messily here in America (7)
20 Happy to rip off the canvas (7)
22 Tens follow speaker of religious musical stories (9)
23 Do they dog people like me? (7)
24 The way everybody could lose control in flight (5)
25 He gets to his feet and postulates (9)

Down

1 Behind the brown hatch I find some Indian cooking (8)
2 A centaur perhaps feeds from the betel palm tree (5-3)
3 Eastern Holland was first to obtain support (6)
4 Is she a fellow? (6)
5 Cast dine hungrily with a certain aloofness (8)
6 Madly adore men - charmed, I'm sure (8)
7 Oddly afraid of said musical pieces (6)
8 Beat about the ears! (6)
14 Logical principle lacking sensible conclusion (8)
15 Double vision (8)
16 It's unnecessary not to want so much (8)
17 Charges hospital department for having stains (8)
18 Reconnoitres for the big cubs (6)
19 First class accountants head over heels about the plant (6)
20 Chico's siesta taken dressed in a bikini, perhaps (6)
21 Talk about the jumper without Jack (6)

74

Across

9 Discover bank holds rand (5)
10 Programme notes (5,4)
11 Carry on with doctor when having a disease! (4,3)
12 Director longed to be made redundant? (7)
13 Fighting that's audible in second part of tennis match (3-2)
14 Dandy lies around, demonstrating sloth maybe (6,3)
16 Releasing strong emotion and whistling in the kitchen? (7,3,5)
19 Slumping, needing reinforcement at end of month (9)
21 Shed in which murderer's hidden body initially (5)
23 Setback destroying pleasure – university admission denied (7)
25 It's clean below North American city to start with (7)
27 Restrains one's daughter in built-up area (5,4)
28 In the finish yours truly gets to improve (5)

Down

1 Female took control and escaped (4)
2 A white substance lying under black rock (6)
3 Woman going to party with old dress on – problem with not being young (4,6)
4 Said to have begun right away (6)
5 Bashful star (3,5)
6 Port remaining in the glass? (4)
7 Table cover needed with proper game being held (8)
8 Lad meaning to become a top performer (7,3)
13 Singleness of purpose as oily dirt is shifted (10)
15 They are at home in Oxford (4,6)
17 Having a go at path over heather (8)
18 His friend may not see him as a beast (5,3)
20 Information about a source of lead and area for its ore (6)

75

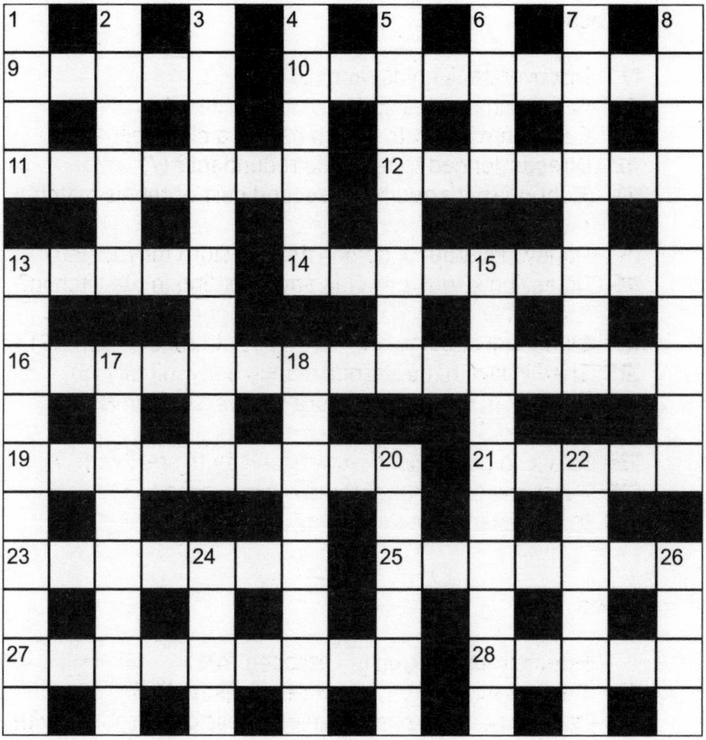

22 Getting ahead of time, shift an amount of money (6)
24 Into gym goes outsize model (4)
26 Journey made by fish under river (4)

Across

1 Dealer starts copying manager (8)
5 No longer available, price reduction for remnant (6)
9 Solid young scout in charge (5)
10 Tall rogue developing into a boorish youth (5,4)
12 Lover not returning to town (10)
13 Jay has one French female for just over four weeks (4)
15 Component part of the electorate (11)
16 Squeeze more than half in vineyard (3)
17 Thanks Penny once for small amount (3)
18 Graduate back in reputable organisation to walk about (11)
20 Going down in the main (4)
21 Sculptures that in France are dignified (10)
24 Herb, continental turned a bright colour (9)
26 Colour to go on (5)
27 No right direction in the country (6)
28 Supposed to have looked forward to an event (8)

Down

1 Small creature found by bounder in American intelligence unit (6)
2 Colour of flashing beam on river (5)
3 Book where it is darkest before dawn (10)
4 Valley to dry up (3)
6 Parting of the ways (4)
7 Cake fried by first two teammates after the game (9)
8 Edward intercepted beast that had taken unsteady steps (8)
10 Made lawful daughter born in wedlock first (11)
11 Person destroying spirit of tax official (11)
14 Almost 10 down, one preying on discerning lawyer (5,5)
15 Ganymede's saucer? (9)
16 It is worn near the Welsh coast (8)
19 Written in confinement (6)

76

22 Search for something in an antique style (5)
23 Lady puts last letter before first on rear admiral (4)
25 She appeared in the very beginning (3)

Across

7 Purge has racist components (9)
8 Dependable form of alloy (5)
10 Motor shells or bodies (8)
11 About to lose, being careless (6)
12 Wharf ripe for demolition (4)
13 Taking someone on of attractive disposition (8)
15 A novel division of the church (7)
17 Risk getting left in church (7)
20 It may be simple to engage one's attention (8)
22 Gravity-free network (4)
25 Il Duce turned out to be a mathematician (6)
26 Change of diet not a remedy (8)
27 Keep silent about mother's accident (5)
28 Sort of sketch one won't want to go under the hammer (9)

Down

1 Sort of speed trap caught girl in posh car (5)
2 Stylish greeting is somewhat affected (6)
3 Jam book under piano (8)
4 I left the priest in church (7)
5 Appropriate weapon for a British private (5,3)
6 Coach may take on ineffective player (9)
9 U.S. prison ship (4)
14 Skinny, toothless what's-his-name (9)
16 Perfect lady about fifty (8)
18 Jolly occasion long overdue (4,4)
19 A whip-round held by the junior diplomat (7)
21 Objects when tips are offered? (4)
23 I ring Enid up for an antiseptic (6)
24 Place for landing and take-off (5)

77

Across

- **1** Bitter on pub floor (6)
- **5** Check glowing piece about new copper (8)
- **9** Native kind ringing Tory leader (10)
- **10** Gripped right and proper (4)
- **11** Respecting air control (8)
- **12** Cane scoundrel with cane (6)
- **13** Fairy queen embraced by Greek character (4)
- **15** Former bird taking almost everything outside (8)
- **18** Big jumper and anorak go together badly (8)
- **19** Fast time on GameCube? (4)
- **21** Pork pie by socialist creates disgust (6)
- **23** Embarrassing fall on one's head! (8)
- **25** Look miserable, we hear (4)
- **26** Liberal daily Independent's on desk (10)
- **27** A French Conservative urgency is immoral (8)
- **28** Notice an abstainer's on edge (6)

Down

- **2** Only an advance, say (5)
- **3** Punting around for example shows breeding (9)
- **4** Dismissal of agreement about Ulster (6)
- **5** Changing tone, Iran elected for alliance (7,8)
- **6** 'Speed' star has no heart (8)
- **7** Excellence of setter on endless form (5)
- **8** Walk along the beach (9)
- **14** Inmate on a disorderly discharge (9)
- **16** Robin and Batman initially held by arrested crook? (9)
- **17** Decries hype in ceasefires (8)
- **20** Pain from pang in arm? (6)
- **22** Spread and controlled by church (5)
- **24** Look in marsh for Magwitch, perhaps (5)

78

Across

1 Member of the clergy over other ranks (6)
4 Humiliating failure concealed by Mafia's controller (6)
8 Save in bank (3)
10 Harsh treatment in bleak wood (3,4)
11 Divine English city, as in novel (7)
12 Current doctor, frightfully fit (5)
13 In succession to throne, displaced head of Tudors (2,3,4)
14 Girl, sad now, upset by grand music hall song (5,4,4)
17 Made envious, an eccentric in the advertising industry (7,6)
22 Without hesitation, ask hotel abroad about one (4,1,4)
23 Swagger in bar (5)
24 Good actress, alluring beauty (7)
25 Scored briskly, a fifty by member run out (7)
26 Knight is backing king (3)
27 French girl, nine, fixing plug (6)
28 Nation securing superior sculpture (6)

Down

1 A padre prepared for a public procession (6)
2 Spotted social reformer in factory (7)
3 Evident throughout time (5)
5 Climber has some distance to go to make US academic circle (3,6)
6 Argue after small child brings one to a squalid quarter (4,3)
7 Decorated knight brought in to give a speech (6)
8 Ruby is concerned about Rex in play (5,8)
9 Meals on wheels provider? (10,3)
14 Branch member (3)
15 On watch in rough part of lower Manhattan (9)
16 Bevan embraced by Anthony Eden (3)
18 Embarrassing week in a hospital room (7)

79

19 Good sort of piano (7)
20 Work hard on an advertising catchphrase (6)
21 Blow for a member of the rowing crew (6)
23 Leave Croatian port (5)

Across

1 Parts of the body designed to bear swords? (8,6)
9 A numeric sort of digital improvement (8)
10 Short time employment for computer worker (5)
12 Runs to help in attack (4)
13 Vehicles that leave marks of injury on bear (6,4)
15 The cleaning lady has a dress, oddly, for these word games (8)
16 Extends studies on central London area (6)
18 Miss the old flipping footman! (6)
20 Left home in American state - to take drugs! (8)
23 Beaten by argument in favour of being put forward (10)
24 Large-scale source of power in melting ice (4)
26 Player's answer to put in credit (5)
27 Leave after disagreement about missing ends (8)
28 Einstein tag ill suits them - not! (14)

Down

2 Croatian lost time fighting this player (7)
3 Both sides welcome first-class accommodation in the wild (4)
4 Supplied crack in deep disguise (8)
5 Clouded over early after bright start (6)
6 Acknowledgements from delegations after a day (10)
7 The compiler went up to university with recent copy (7)
8 Resist changes in coinage with tenacity (11)
11 Waspish couple reportedly got fruit (7,4)
14 Ethnic group studies Ascot, for example (10)
17 Cold call about a note supplying the necessaries (8)
19 One's in the soup after Tory accepted resounding defeat (7)
21 Road up on favourite American drive (7)
22 A French source of water that makes you sick (6)
25 Three points about river bird (4)

80

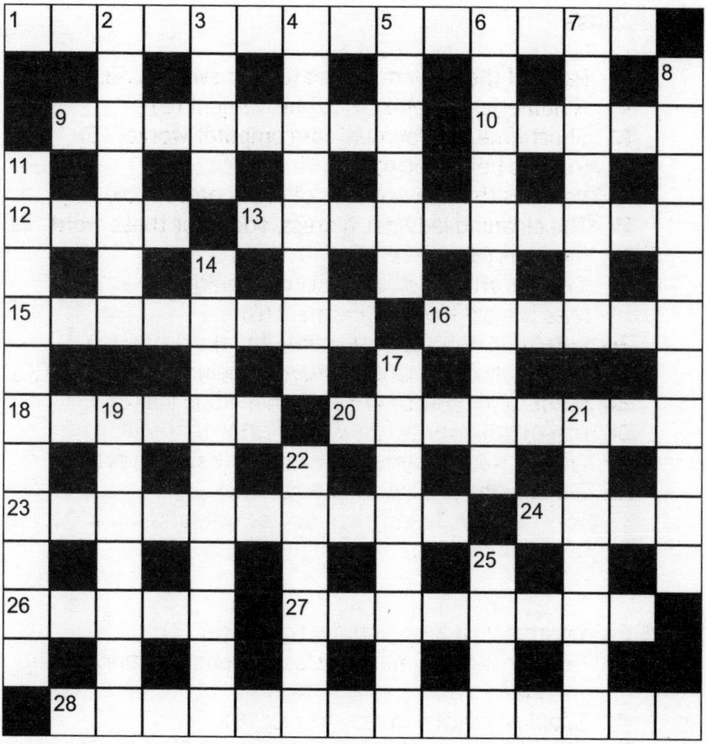

Across

1 Are pasties too much for meal? Yes (6)
4 Stop by customs buildings (6)
8 Endless anger when this coat is seen? (3)
10 Gosh! Bill is knocked back by this island! (7)
11 The result of synchronising watches once (3-4)
12 One of two ancient writers given work outside home (5)
13 When perhaps to be uncouth (5-4)
14 Banking centre – one involved in many scandals, sadly (6,7)
17 Swanking, having great reputation (13)
22 Like a sort of check on patterned board (9)
23 Bread for a bird (5)
24 Row about upper-class B&B offering more fat (7)
25 Minister's place about to take on two Conservatives (7)
26 See bank beginning to disappear (3)
27 Bury hospital department doctor with nothing to gain (6)
28 Financial dealer could be bankrupt, right? (6)

Down

1 Distraught epicure rejecting university kitchen's formula (6)
2 The first section includes Italian piece of music (7)
3 Very High-Church and holy, absorbed by the heavens above (5)
5 In charge of animals, reportedly – as picked up by snooper? (9)
6 Bread arriving at No 25? (7)
7 Area below hard bones (6)
8 Honest description of old-fashioned blonde (4,3,6)
9 Place for the hanging of criminals? (6,7)
14 Company good for one of its less important workers? (3)
15 Peculiar style of fellow leading miners astray (9)
16 Fuel to rise and sink (3)

81

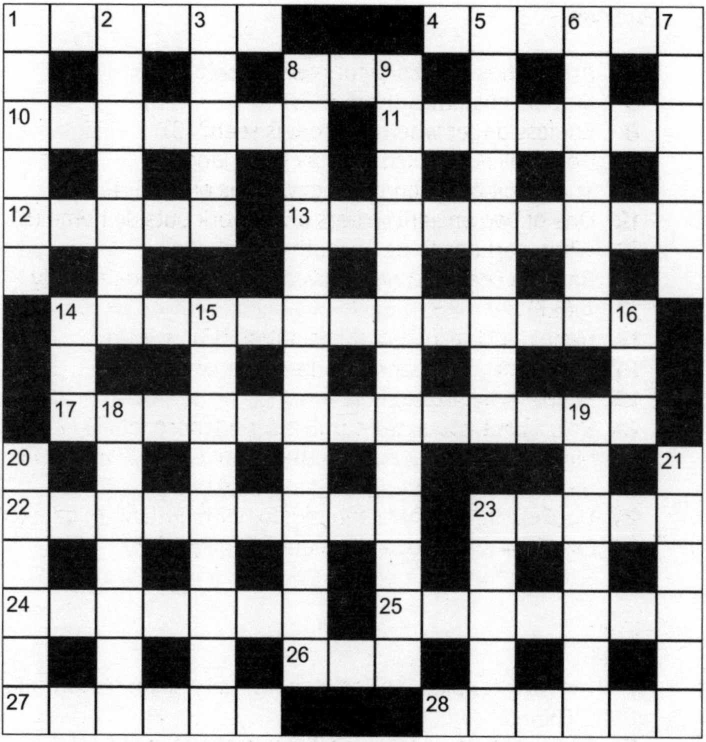

18 Unusual coin found in dish (7)
19 Group of people in employment at computer? (7)
20 Botanical growth of the spring before (6)
21 'Barman' ? (6)
23 Priest stables excellent horse (5)

Across

1 Catch one's breath seeing end of long snake (4)
3 Method of transmitting letters by air – or by foot? (6-4)
8 Timothy reported lively young man also in town in Africa (8)
9 Many a feature concerning gripping accessory (4-2)
10 Independent politician, his undoing is being full of mischief (6)
11 Applaud some reversible flashy display (8)
13 Aim to put electric cable by boundary (4-4)
14 Had an ambition during the night perhaps (6)
16 Very gently put paper inside electronic device (6)
19 Young ladies after short time had syrup (8)
21 Dwarf beautiful woman, one on the wagon inside (8)
22 Lady returning after six in the city (6)
23 Measure emblem on right-hand side of flag (6)
24 He aims for the bull (8)
25 One who is very much the marrying kind (10)
26 Scottish theologian came from this fort in the USA (4)

Down

1 Climbing – out of bed? (7,2)
2 People not an asset when it comes to insurance (6,9)
3 Asiatic vegetable OK with a chip that had been cooked! (3,4)
4 Turn up gold on revolutionary watercolour (7)
5 Old church with troublesome fruit-trees (7)
6 Blunt comment that did not have to be said! (9,6)
7 Some phaeton, uphill, travelling very fast (3-2)
12 Intention of one during the early hours (3)
15 She has a will of her own (9)
17 About to include round eggs (3)
18 Favourite lady introduced single flower (7)
19 Graduate tries replacing masters (7)

82

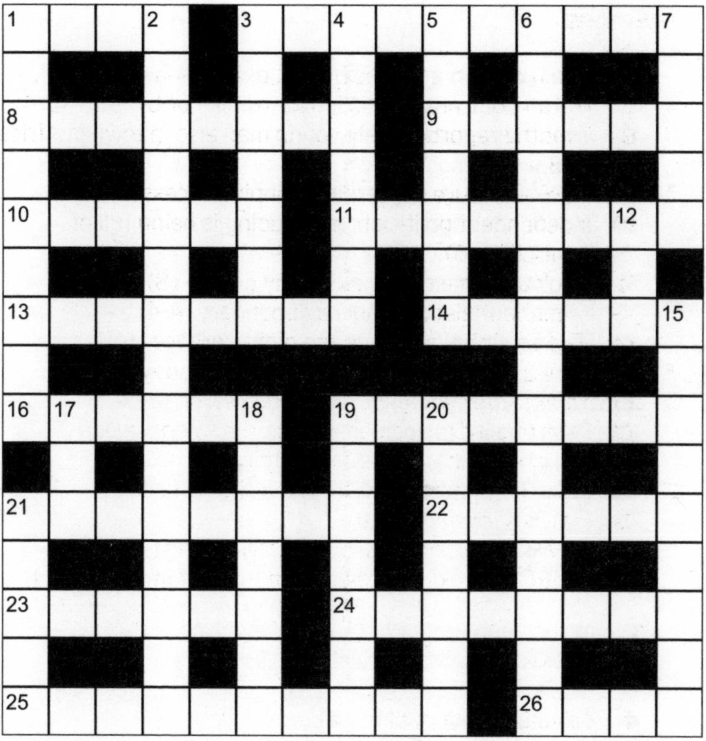

20 Animal at all times allowed out (7)
21 Be left inside with record, high-pitched signal (5)

Across

1 What an igloo provides is poor solace (4,7)
9 The price of silence? (4,5)
10 Musical tea break about six (5)
11 A heavenly model (6)
12 False encouragement given on debts (8)
13 Work's returning, employ a partner (6)
15 Royalty's own touch of honour (8)
18 Breakdown specialists? (8)
19 Note the world shortage (6)
21 Not the straight and narrow path for U.S. entertainment (8)
23 Illicitly acquired bundle of pound notes (6)
26 Object made of spare string (5)
27 Showing a bit of backbone in game (9)
28 Game for some drunken flirting? (11)

Down

1 In such agreement cash, too, is involved (7)
2 Runner defeated in close race (5)
3 Unwilling to go into print (6-3)
4 Be careful – it's said to be booby-trapped (4)
5 Small company simply involved in producing games (8)
6 The one to right of them (5)
7 Club money that is short (7)
8 Extinct animal is around in changed form (8)
14 One who talks one round to composing musical drama (8)
16 Defeat comes from fielding error (9)
17 Bound to be short of cash (8)
18 He will try to cook rarebit (7)
20 They are engaged in outdoor pursuits (7)
22 Number on watch? (5)
24 Left port carrying cargo (5)
25 Our hall is regularly used for exam (4)

83

Across

7 Anxious new bride with stud (9)
8 Stop working for tycoon (5)
10 A file traps weapon scaremonger (8)
11 Croaky hack's heard (6)
12 Bird's bottom, say (4)
13 In seances, trying to find forebears (8)
15 Stony after day on a trip? (7)
17 Rover's rough coat, we hear (7)
20 Close and far off outside? (8)
22 Second place is top (4)
25 Excellent guess (6)
26 Former wife playing tough (8)
27 Initially it's normally gold, oblong typically (5)
28 Perfect place for a quick break? (4,5)

Down

1 Party includes Liberal creep (5)
2 Over-formality leading church (6)
3 Make one rattier, possibly (8)
4 Nervous about Tory leader being bland (7)
5 Idiot runs around and worries (8)
6 Force from criminals on locomotive (9)
9 Bird's endlessly stylish (4)
14 Celebrated in bar till drunk (9)
16 Camp, so raring to revamp (8)
18 Able Scot's tricky snag... (8)
19 ...prosper containing socialist apathy (7)
21 Source of river's up (4)
23 Wrong place for old fags, not hot? (6)
24 End for King Charles' mistress (5)

84

Across

7 Nag getting endless injury? Lowest point recalled (8)
9 Young dog favoured and controlled by others (6)
10 Good scope for farmhouse (6)
11 Hole case developed? Get fastener (8)
12 In all cases like a chess player's moves? (6-3-5)
15 Short break, we hear, for hands (4)
17 Cowboys congregate here in Lutheran church (5)
19 Slippery fellows in parts of ship missing at first (4)
20 Silly chap confused by role for dessert (10,4)
23 A game that builds characters? (8)
25 Fearful woman making advance without leading pair (6)
27 Actor's wandering voyage? (6)
28 Man emerging from scrape in African country (8)

Down

1 Reasonable trade show (4)
2 Read further about boy quickly (6)
3 Responsibility concerning superpower (4)
4 See apparently first doctor showing coolness (6)
5 Something that's shed from second rifle (8)
6 Local CID indisciplined after training? Not a major fault! (10)
8 Medical helper and doctor on new series I missed (7)
13 Shopping facility? Cleaner, say, turns up with comb (6,4)
14 Pivotal point in teaching ethics (5)
16 Scattered crop said to grow wild (8)
18 Talk tiresomely about old spear (7)
21 Sign shown by male beneath limitless football stadium (6)
22 Stiff class attended by a learner (6)
24 Drink up around British island (4)
26 Shady operator upset bigwigs (4)

85

Across

1 Father, for example, welcomes post being returned to the house (10)
6 Set fund taking the odds for stallion (4)
9 One paid out to chase worker from the South (10)
10 Cries of pain over lake birds (4)
13 Said something after son followed (7)
15 There's nothing in Turner to dislike (6)
16 A swindle by outwardly divine man of the church (6)
17 To separately live is such (5,10)
18 Firm desire to return before Sunday – the rabbits! (6)
20 Worry about show of hesitation for search (6)
21 The ruler lost time in anger, getting nothing right (7)
22 One working on student is an animal (4)
25 The ceremony in which company people welcome private soldiers (10)
26 Fill in forms at election (4)
27 His drug den is shaky! (10)

Down

1 Answer found in favourite fuel (4)
2 Ceremony that's correct for the listeners (4)
3 One unable to speak about quiet attribute (6)
4 Average White Band on the way? (6-2-3-4)
5 Want to take a run, and got close (6)
7 News presenters broadcast rector's win (4,6)
8 Cleans up CID fitness to operate (10)
11 Finishes welcoming visit, and escapes (5,5)
12 Dropping unconscious, and breaking ranks (7,3)
13 Close look at sleep? (4-3)
14 Free of French meat (7)
19 Urbane and married in comfort, mostly (6)
20 Seek food seeing kid captured by the enemy (6)
23 Car that's at home in the road (4)
24 Weapons are raised, to be comfortable (4)

86

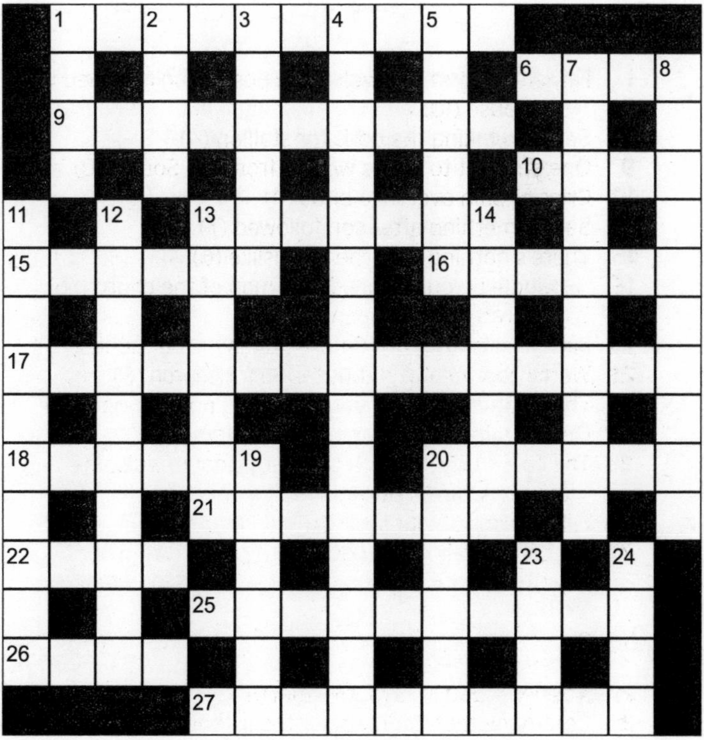

Across

1 Negotiator gets the password wrong (4,7)
8 Female performer – I chant, doing a maths exercise (11)
11 Noise one doesn't give if not bothered (4)
12 Weight system in old city (4)
13 Less significant fit of temper before row (7)
15 Some men, thus excited, wax lyrical (7)
16 Big noise and little man had food and drink (5)
17 Hesitation when meeting big Greek god (4)
18 A mother's boy (4)
19 Brown salt water – very good for drinking! (5)
21 Ineffectual person has gone mad, showing deep resentment (7)
22 English politician to be in debt to Queen giving sanction (7)
23 Right name given at end of story (4)
26 Participant in Boat Race puffed audibly (4)
27 Sort of hymn – carol is seen to be different (11)
28 Disagreement continued with travellers to end of day (11)

Down

2 Some of the athletes in preliminary race (4)
3 Initially partner was irritated, being chucked (7)
4 Lake – see sailor heading north (4)
5 Day when gun is carried in London area (4,3)
6 Harangue worker after end of labour (4)
7 Designer finds fault with implement, leading to depression (11)
8 Subordinate worker who won't get taken for a ride? (4,7)
9 Reason we will put down for gathering movement (11)
10 Enormous shop there – my park is ruined (11)
14 Split, like a vehicle in motion losing its front (5)

87

15 Weird emanation's beginning to descend on lake (5)
19 Able to pay out for a chemical (7)
20 A peculiarly sombre saint (7)
24 Sea captain has upset little old fellows (4)
25 Look after seaman in port (4)
26 Prevents from entering pub rooms (4)

Across

1 Boring way of discovering success and wealth (8,3)
7 Article left out of treatise rewritten in port (7)
8 Friendly understanding that could be more than cordial (7)
10 Title had initially been put in ramshackle display (8)
11 Various cuts made by commander on plaster (6)
13 Look out for said believer (4)
14 Dispense these days with one in church (10)
16 Taken from photo no longer obtainable from publisher (3,2,5)
18 Spots Bill, one without the ball (4)
21 Break in to repair rupture located within (6)
22 Eccentric named Ron having been sent back into custody (2,6)
24 Press used on only half a garment? (7)
25 Dilatory perhaps, nothing missing lately (7)
26 Would digging give him a healthy appetite? (11)

Down

1 Many yarns have been spun about it (7)
2 During the interval is to oppose (6)
3 Leave the light off when one has to conceal something (4,2,4)
4 Leo North came up at the present time (4)
5 Barely beat one's opponents? (8)
6 Design etched on floor-covering first (7)
7 One who takes the long view (11)
9 Green on the same side is not threatening the environment (11)
12 Get men in to vandalise plant! (10)
15 Softie travelling about freezing-point in a type of skiing (3-5)
17 Get rid of grass in the pavilion (4,3)
19 Tribe surrounding city had old trumpet (7)

88

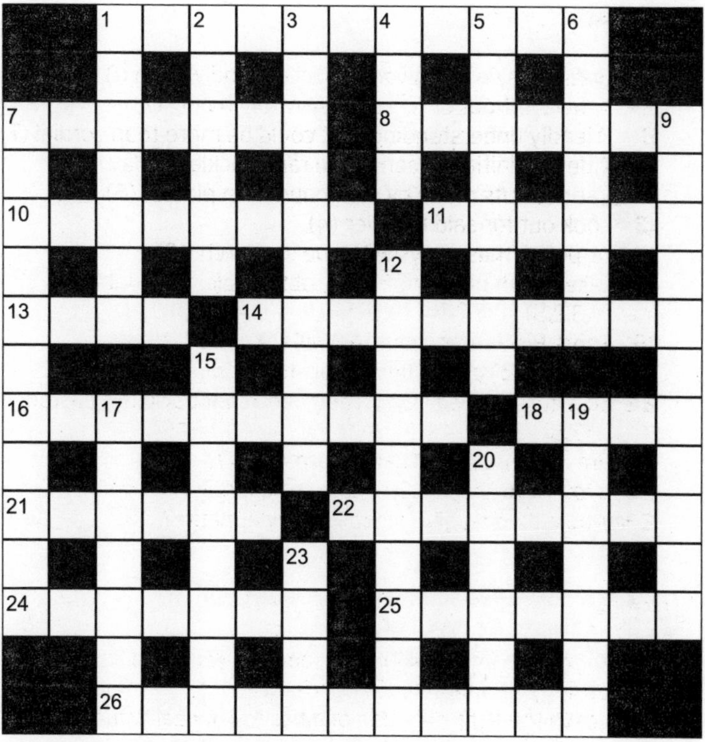

20 Diminutive lady going over the edge with vertigo (6)
23 Heather loses a man (4)

Across

1 Corresponding but never meeting (8)
6 Father quick to get high religious office (6)
9 Where gambling is a bad thing in company (6)
10 Tea with fine china is delightful (8)
11 Exist on next to nothing, being humble (8)
12 Field a ball, perhaps (6)
13 Recollection of events in crime scene reconstruction (12)
16 As produced by air-liners? (6,6)
19 Kipling character to watch out, in short (6)
21 One convinced there's possible evil in drink (8)
23 A well-known symphony, also part of variation (8)
24 As a whole where diplomats excel (6)
25 Does the writing for another Ibsen play (6)
26 Means hail-storms, perhaps (8)

Down

2 A new stage setting may include them (6)
3 This excuse is out of place (5)
4 I'm on later performing at the circus (4-5)
5 Stand for a lesson (7)
6 Soundly commend what a churchgoer does (5)
7 Publications that are rarely bound to sell (9)
8 Yet it may help a company to expand (8)
13 Finishes on the board in lodging house as sleeping partners (4,5)
14 Painting that lacks humanity? (5,4)
15 A wave of reaction (8)
17 Polish girl with German complaint (7)
18 Possibly secure and free from danger (6)
20 Stories with a twist to them? (5)
22 Another run (5)

89

Across

4 One who assists with lateral pass in football? (8)
8 Constant increases producing very difficult times (6)
9 Poetry about an artist from Italian city (8)
10 Medicine provided by clergyman about four (8)
11 Composer of dance in major key, initially (6)
12 Girl's capital in 14 (8)
13 Dilatory reforms believed in by nobody in good faith? (8)
16 Source of white blossom, as American author said (8)
19 Counter-argument that's genuine about central target (8)
21 New bowler, for example, is not so stale (3,3)
23 Snake seen on Indian's foot (8)
24 Ideal partner providing what sounds like only way to end game (8)
25 Courageous about current, most of the time (6)
26 With skill, converted from 13 (8)

Down

1 Justification for land that goes with house (7)
2 Stalin as a crazy aggressor (9)
3 Charlie is covering one in place of Francis (6)
4 Great treatment! In dose, every germ destroyed (9,6)
5 Businessman – the guy who makes decisions about cuts (8)
6 Form of Oriental fighting getting encouragement from Barbie? (5)
7 Accountant not as outgoing as bank worker (7)
14 Gore in part of Europe, or another continent (9)
15 Reduce formal agreement between parties (8)
17 Everything being included, implying end of story? (3,4)
18 Artist with musical instrument getting reduced fare from Italy (7)
20 Alter into suit (6)
22 Man will ring – and hear this? (5)

90

Across

9 Girl over in Latin America (5)
10 Actor, terrible at reading (9)
11 Basically, a nasty threat (2,5)
12 Long curl of hair enclosed in covering letter (7)
13 Greek starter (5)
14 Accountant's girl - her forecasts were never believed (9)
16 Chance to meet him acting in play (3,6,6)
19 Military command given by class members (5,4)
21 Unenthusiastic in assembly about carrying piano (5)
23 Several books in one vehicle (7)
25 Policeman arresting husband with axe (7)
27 Ivy, perhaps, always growing (9)
28 Search around a resort (5)

Down

1 Silence army's leader, unable to think clearly (4)
2 Board member, church dignitary (6)
3 Girl in car on a cliff pointing to island (10)
4 Constant interference? (6)
5 He played with J Lennon spending hour with troops (8)
6 Put article in study for faculty head (4)
7 Drive out from Diane's cottage (8)
8 Not married? Let loose! (10)
13 Expert on moving house? (10)
15 One's got one (10)
17 Threaten to close, wind up (8)
18 More than one crack shot targets soldiers (8)
20 Back in a tick (6)
22 Leave briefly to get river fish (3,3)
24 Plenty of trousers (4)
26 Legal documents read out for Swiss hotelier (4)

91

Across

1 The Persians worried about this (for example) (11)
9 Bird that's additional to Indian dish (9)
10 Ideal type has to be handled (5)
11 Rocky road to home rule (6)
12 Fish out of water? (8)
13 Was sick after hospital called (6)
15 Fire enveloping new pub and cafe (5-3)
18 Preparation for exam on imagination (8)
19 Strong marijuana – about half a score (6)
21 Determined defenders are disadvantages (8)
23 One when taken over by France's top company is a disaster (6)
26 Fast? Old and slow! (5)
27 A symptom of hot love? (9)
28 Suitable paper tip, or a mixture thereof (11)

Down

1 Non-u pub involved with choir music (7)
2 Dominated and was in front after the game (5)
3 Curiosity about one quality of sound (9)
4 Circular band needed for house work (4)
5 Turning on the charm? (8)
6 University supporting depressed Hindu leader and holy man (5)
7 Supplier of food who's a queen among queens! (7)
8 Liberal may be heard, we hear – that's commendable! (8)
14 Soliciting would be provoking if five became a hundred (8)
16 Church Tories misinterpreted right to have one singing (9)
17 Labour's bound to be in here! (8)
18 Whispers of regulations covering the road (7)

92

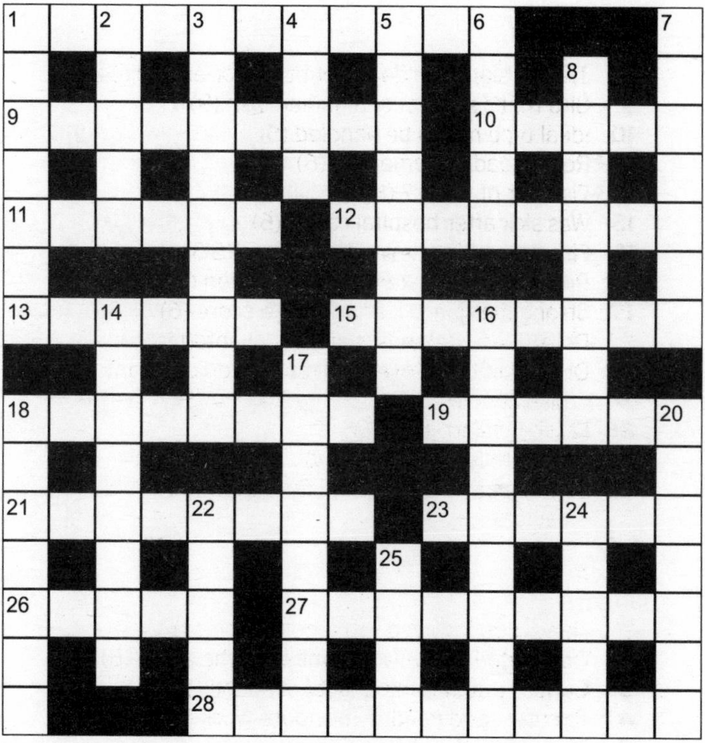

20 Lightweight under alternative Tory whip (7)
22 Greeting a 25, perhaps? (5)
24 Room in Lufthansa unaffected? (5)
25 Ring house to accommodate a student (4)

Across

1 Insects react badly when colliding with posts (12)
9 Depressed women entertained by fellow (4)
10 Postboy possibly producing confusion – awfully green? (9)
12 Superior fur, not yet ready for being chucked out (6)
13 Tom's about to go round Irish county (8)
15 One may sit on the board of an eating establishment (5,5)
16 Country lads getting nothing for duke (4)
18 A girl meeting a premature end unfortunately (4)
20 Child tucking into Lancashire dish, child making a mess (10)
23 Ready to drop, like a boxer? (3-5)
24 Character dispatched communication (6)
26 Fail to be alarmed? (9)
27 Foreign ruler and Queen going over motorway (4)
28 Someone who used to like farm vehicle's ventilation device (9,3)

Down

2 Worms can make wiggly line in shifting sand (8)
3 Eastern male married a girl (4)
4 To scoff pie is naughty in a public building (4,6)
5 Story to introduce the German songs (6)
6 Golf course where ace is seen at end of month (7)
7 So "ether's part" could fancifully be this? (12)
8 Prepare herb for fixed amount of medicine (6)
11 Was it lost when Mrs Hubbard failed to deliver? (8,4)
14 Unintelligible in company, he will get torn apart (10)
17 They don't last long and may be thrown into mere heap (8)
19 Increase gold given to American agents over time (7)
21 Bird nibbled morsel of bread maybe (6)
22 Party is loud – afternoon rest unable to begin (6)
25 Box left over is incomplete (4)

93

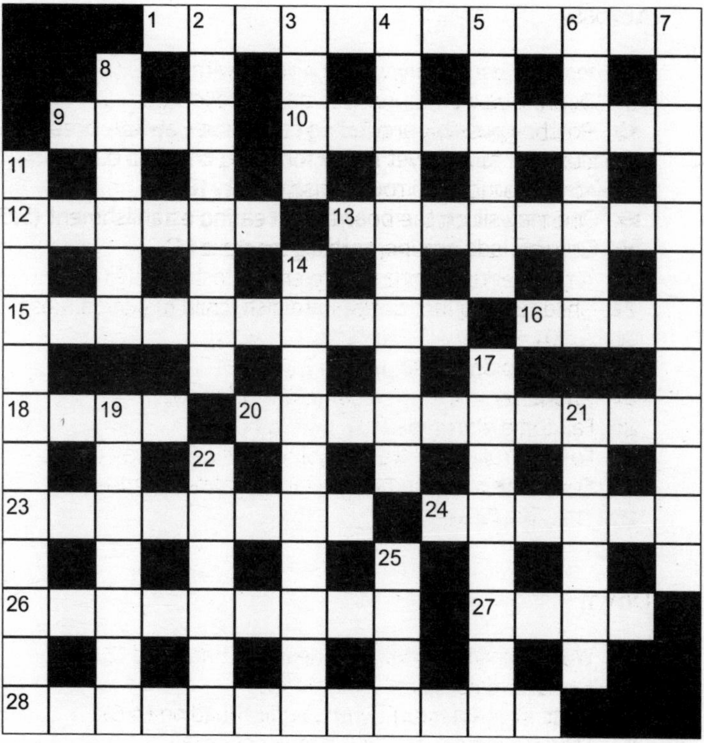

Across

1 One soon becomes angry with it (5,6)
9 Turning point (5)
10 Reach the German suffering loss of rights (9)
11 Outside dilapidated flat (7)
12 Very dark aeroplane that cannot be seen at night? (3-5)
14 One's kept in the shade – that's a troublesome thing (8)
15 Knot on tree inside trunk narrowed (4)
17 Girl, Virginia, going round a loch (7)
19 Sauce placed in front of one of these beans (4)
20 Generate fizzy drink! (5,3)
21 Self-abasement gripped last character in Cornish resort (8)
23 Saint finds his station in London (7)
25 Price of silence? (4,5)
26 Rod, pole or perch (5)
27 Felt knowledgeable (11)

Down

2 Get knotted? Just the reverse (5)
3 Order into tea room (7)
4 Lady included clown stopping short in Africa (8)
5 Left afloat (4)
6 Cecilia was in Africa? (8)
7 No icing to be removed whilst in disguise (9)
8 Newly sealed variety of cheese (11)
12 Jesting a bit in all seriousness (6,5)
13 Keen to remove cover from one's leg (7)
16 Time when following number are performing (9)
17 Hold in deep respect, are turning up during new event (8)
18 Take someone aboard against their will from 5 (8)
19 Bath from the past, about now! (3,4)
22 Junction eight, say (5)
24 Store to give away (4)

94

Across

1 Please request a re-trial (6)
4 Send away for being a complete failure (5,3)
9 Sports trunks? (6)
10 Sense there's agreement among a number (8)
12 It's unusual to return right on time (4)
13 Silly mistake artfully hidden (5)
14 Kind of bender the vanquished go on (4)
17 High concept that failed due to bad communications (5,2,5)
20 It is there for the asking (8-4)
23 Spot for parking inside, yes? Possibly (4)
24 Top man in building trade left during a row (5)
25 Workman in stone (4)
28 Fat, and very wet (8)
29 Putting spirit into a severe beating (6)
30 Ridicule deal in the clothing business (3,5)
31 Agreeable question (3,3)

Down

1 Account supported by a clergyman should be reliable (8)
2 A local tour (3,5)
3 Size of field for a medley-race? (4)
5 Israel army on manoeuvres are jolly fellows! (5,7)
6 Model to apply for a job (4)
7 Musical journals? (6)
8 Stout female's parent (6)
11 Traditional cocktail? (3-9)
15 Very pleased with oneself – being so outstanding? (5)
16 Intends to give me a short answer (5)
18 Drive a camping convertible (8)
19 Star as a roof-raiser? (8)
21 Principal meets queen in dive (6)
22 Procure release of prisoner before summer (6)

95

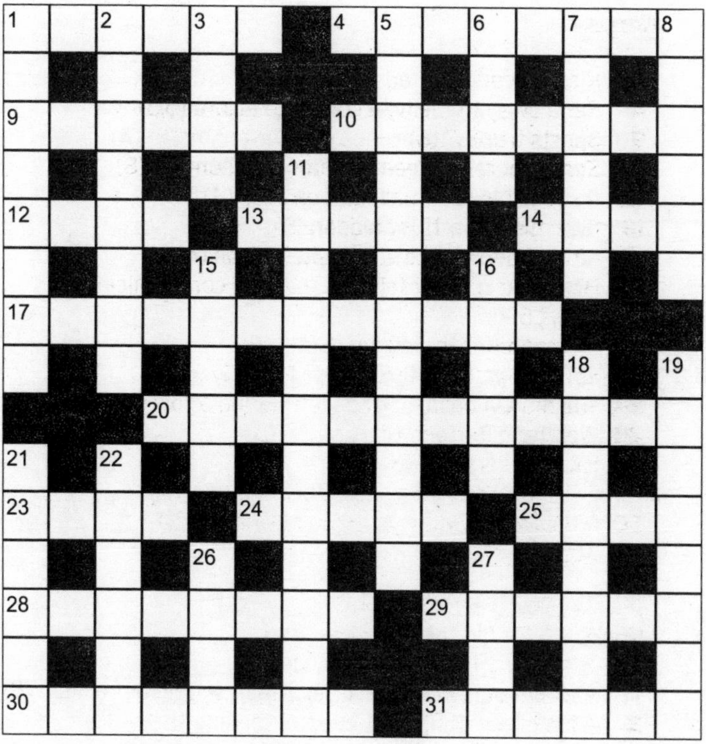

26 Practise boxing in the yard (4)
27 Not considered a disfigurement (4)

Across

7 Crumbling bone found in tumulus? (8)
9 Country with one's fabled King returning (6)
10 Success ends following compiler confusion (4)
11 Continuing pollution includes America (10)
12 Hard idiot the French torment (6)
14 Sold grass containing dock (8)
15 In theatre morphine produces shock (6)
17 This clue is a pain! (6)
20 Laws of time in figures (8)
22 Boring commercials for spirits (6)
23 Enormous, fantastic treat in box (10)
24 Sailor new on lake (4)
25 Scoffed after pub? It's natural (6)
26 Console dying? (8)

Down

1 Crest of a wave tip (8)
2 Long for girl (4)
3 Kitty catching head of ugly dog (6)
4 Carried out work in charge of teaching (8)
5 Short-lived Conservative after terrible strain (10)
6 Where happy medium may be found? (6)
8 Abandon fool perhaps, losing heart (6)
13 Strong test on Iran resolution (10)
16 Got into bed drunk around one (8)
18 Madrid, say, chasing team of stars (8)
19 Literary lion initially terribly oblique (6)
21 Burdensome Tory leader withdrawing (6)
22 Old fogey's knees-up, endlessly slow (6)
24 Get a bit of stick? (4)

96

Across

1 Breaks down, strangely enough (6,2)
6 It may go down well, but one dies to kick it (6)
9 Entertainment that's a nice change to mother (6)
10 Woman's habit is to delay, that is the end of it (8)
11 The longest chord in non-musical circles (8)
12 Throw out uneven and inferior material (6)
13 An angel-fish? Gracious! (4,8)
16 Looks forward to having the last word in pickles (12)
19 I'm taking a certain attitude for tax (6)
21 A competition to fire people (4-4)
23 Expires, broken by a wager, and disease (8)
24 Marital relations (2-4)
25 Stevenson's better half (6)
26 Artist is to become a writer (8)

Down

2 Fruit is gathered in the fall (6)
3 The best Religious Education received in academic stream (5)
4 Know-all rascal met trouble (5,4)
5 He's bound to seek a religious goal (7)
6 Extra good for French to meet American (5)
7 Tribe seek to rise under many a brave leader (9)
8 He's wicked to make lover die in a nasty way (4-4)
13 Baffled hounds bark for water guarded by Labrador (6,3)
14 He doesn't volunteer to study the text (9)
15 Track from the terminal (4-4)
17 Broods about one's exploits (7)
18 Shows displeasure seeing the brotherhood on board (6)
20 Speak well of former lover to first lover (5)
22 Man who may impose a rigid measure? (5)

97

Across

1 Accusation in glib eloquent fashion (5)
4 Spotted having kiss in toboggan (8)
8 Dared to have used this capital before day begins (8)
9 Clay Rita modelled with cheerful readiness (8)
11 Edward hides the hide (7)
13 Alumnus criticises said debts that are offensive (9)
15 Horse pulling barge, one is reliable (5,2,8)
18 Recorder found main point during rarer excitement (9)
21 Water that is crystalline in form! (7)
22 Lady put articles behind broken door (8)
24 Had nothing more than stew during battle (8)
25 Thus, say, am finding raw material behind tree (8)
26 Mistakenly link up most of spaceship (5)

Down

1 Pointless communication? (4-6)
2 Stop a humble building (8)
3 Left relative who did not start the hilarity (8)
4 Thus US barman has to add this to whisky (4)
5 Bone male bird number six reportedly found (6)
6 US immigrant from Los Angeles can take nothing (6)
7 Drug found inside parched nest (4)
10 Unlikely to appeal to schoolchildren for a considerable time (4-4)
12 Refer to surprising inclusion of round ridgepole (8)
14 Volume of students? (6,4)
16 Still decline after the end of the afternoon (8)
17 Daily with minor responsibilities (8)
19 Gary interminably licked half of pungent root (6)
20 Sergeant-major includes it with company programme (6)
22 Lady stops short of podium (4)
23 One outspoken lady (4)

98

Across

7 Lucky yet strange turn o' fate (9)
8 No head on the beer? That is strange (5)
10 Out to the opening ball from a spin-bowler (3-5)
11 They fight with one another (6)
12 Lover's knot, say (4)
13 Arrived in a bundle (6,2)
15 Multiply without going forth (7)
17 Branches of the animal kingdom (7)
20 Paid cricketer placed in a deep position (8)
22 Whistle a hit? (4)
25 A rendezvous lined with trees (6)
26 Switch choices occasionally (2,3,3)
27 A fibre preparation, not long-lasting (5)
28 Thrills with loose woman get things moving (9)

Down

1 Foals are frisky after a tonic, perhaps (3-2)
2 Wound up the Spanish firm (6)
3 In very short time the river becomes unsafe (8)
4 Men in the firing line (7)
5 Two sources of surprise (4,4)
6 Cavalryman, an expert swimmer (9)
9 Post filled by a knight? (4)
14 Dog entered in races is withdrawn (9)
16 Put more money in or gave some back (8)
18 A banker's order in America (8)
19 I cooked it with cod, I must be daft! (7)
21 Customs applications (4)
23 At work, - but raising no tax (2,4)
24 A point about wood for burning (5)

99

Across

1 Arrive at the position indicated in the middle of the page (4,2,6)
8 Swirling lasso without a tail (5)
9 Spices that he smuggles inside vehicles (9)
11 Bury before trouble starts to unfold (9)
12 Commonly named forger (5)
13 Roaming in Devon, he ended up in the Netherlands! (9)
16 A soggy old grub (5)
18 Even again, Daddy's light-headed (5)
19 Characteristic behaviour is masculine (9)
20 The beer on the right is active (5)
22 Shows that registers include a central tritone (9)
25 Support for Laurel's Chinese charge (9)
26 Classify alien without a special translator (5)
27 Selena whined about such publicity (4,8)

Down

1 A hundred rushed around but were eventually restrained (9)
2 Runner starts marathon in London, eagerly racing (5)
3 Out, worthy cat? No, suffer quite the opposite (5)
4 Ironstone employed as a neurotransmitter (9)
5 Form a friend at school (9)
6 Anna omitted to include mention of being Ruth's mother-in-law (5)
7 Dirty window pane often found in church (7,5)
10 Fishy captain is in form (12)
14 Piles of grass chimneys (9)
15 Uncoiled viper aims to play the bloodsucker (9)
17 Exit scene to regain ones livelihood (9)
21 Steer clear of lady now in (5)
23 Fed up with the study I'd turned upside down (5)
24 Crikey! Soldier has short legs, for example (5)

100

Solutions

Solutions 1-3

1

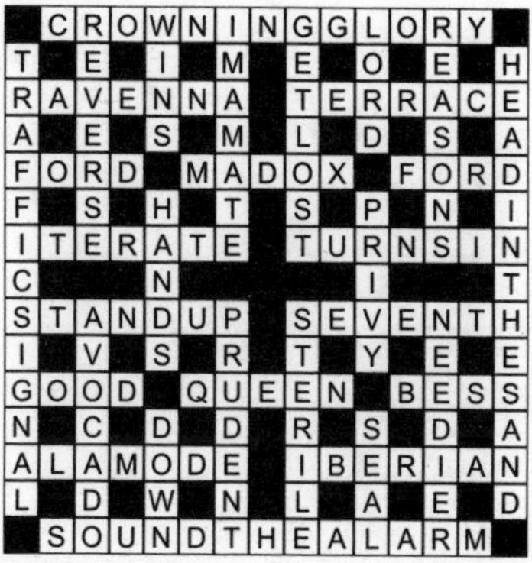

2

3

Solutions 4-6

4

M	A	S	S	M	A	R	K	E	T		J	A	M	B
O		O		A		E		X				P		I
S	E	A	L	I	N	G	W	A	X		G	O	N	G
T		R		N		I		C		S		L		B
			K	E	Y	O	F	T	H	E	D	O	O	R
S		L		N		N		I		Q		G		O
T	W	E	N	T	Y		D	O	C	U	M	E	N	T
I		A		R		B		N		E		T		H
R	A	D	I	A	T	O	R		A	S	S	I	Z	E
R		G		N		T		M		T		C		R
U	G	L	Y	C	U	S	T	O	M	E	R			
P		A		E		W		R		R		V		E
C	O	N	Y		F	A	N	A	T	I	C	I	S	M
U		C				N		S		N		E		M
P	R	E	Y		P	A	S	S	A	G	E	W	A	Y

5

A	C	U	P	U	N	C	T	U	R	E				T
L		S		N		R		S		N		A		H
G	L	A	D	S	T	O	N	E		N	O	U	S	E
E		G		H		P		F		U		D		A
R	E	E	L	E	D		P	U	G	I	L	I	S	T
I				A				L				E		R
A	E	R	A	T	E		A	L	L	I	A	N	C	E
		E		H		P		Y		N		C		
C	O	Q	U	E	T	R	Y		S	T	R	E	A	M
A		U				O				H				E
B	R	I	G	A	N	D	S		T	E	T	H	E	R
R		T		I		U		E		C		A		I
A	H	E	A	D		C	I	V	I	L	L	I	S	T
N		D		E		E		E		U		F		E
K				S	P	R	I	N	G	B	O	A	R	D

6

	A		C		I		D				H		S	
R	E	M	A	I	N	D	E	R		S	E	W	E	R
	S		S		V		N		S		R		V	
H	O	L	I	N	E	S	S		L	O	C	K	E	R
	P		N		I		I		A		U		N	
		L	O	N	G		T	E	M	P	L	A	T	E
	P				L		Y				E		E	
B	R	I	S	K	E	T		C	H	A	S	T	E	N
	O		A				I		A				N	
A	G	O	N	I	S	E	S		R	A	S	H		
	N		C		T		O		A		O		A	
S	O	R	T	I	E		L	A	N	G	U	I	S	H
	S		I		W		A		G		R		S	
B	I	G	O	T		S	T	A	U	N	C	H	E	R
	S		N				E		E		E		T	

Solutions 7-9

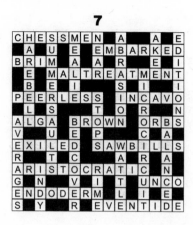

7

C	H	E	S	S	M	E	N		A			A		E
	A		U		E		E	M	B	A	R	K	E	D
B	R	I	M		A		A		R			E		I
	E		M	A	L	T	R	E	A	T	M	E	N	T
	B		E		I				S		I			I
P	E	E	R	L	E	S	S		I	N	C	A	V	O
	L		S				T		O		R			N
A	L	G	A		B	R	O	W	N		O	R	B	S
V			U		E		P				C		A	
E	X	I	L	E	D		S	A	W	B	I	L	L	S
R			T		C				A		R		A	
A	R	I	S	T	O	C	R	A	T	I	C		N	
G		N			V		I		T		U	N	C	O
E	N	D	O	D	E	R	M		L		I		E	
S		Y			R		E	V	E	N	T	I	D	E

8

		H	O	R	S	D	E	C	O	M	B	A	T	
E		E		E		O		A		U		L		
V	A	L	U	I	N	G		D	E	T	R	A	I	N
E		I		N		E		E		A		M		O
N	I	C	O	S	I	A		T	A	B	L	E	A	U
I		A		I		T				L		D		V
N	Y	L	O	N		D	E	P	R	E	C	A	T	E
G						O		I						A
D	E	M	A	G	O	G	U	E		S	A	D	H	U
R		E		R				C		U		E		R
E	N	C	L	A	V	E		E	F	F	E	N	D	I
S		C		N		X		M		F		I		C
S	E	A	M	I	S	T		E	P	I	T	A	P	H
		N		T		R		A		C		L		E
	P	O	L	E	V	A	U	L	T	E	R	S		

9

		S	I	G	H	T	R	E	A	D	E	R		
		T		U		E		P		A		A		
S	W	A	R	M		M	Y	S	T	I	F	I	E	D
L		F		T		P		O		L		S		E
I	N	F	E	R	N	O		M	A	I	D	E	N	S
P		R		E		R				E				P
P	O	O	L	E		I	R	O	N	S	T	O	N	E
E		O				S		V				F		R
D	A	M	A	S	C	E	N	E		M	A	F	I	A
D				T				R		A		L		T
I	N	D	I	A	N	S		M	A	R	T	I	N	I
S		E		D		H		A		R		M		O
C	O	N	T	I	N	E	N	T		O	R	I	O	N
		I		U		B		C		W		T		
		S	Y	M	P	A	T	H	I	S	E	S		

Solutions 10-12

10

TABLECLOTH EVIL
A E X E H O Y
COLLECTION GLEN
K O C T U O C X
LINKUP OSCULATE
E G T R A T N Y
COMEINTOLINE
S W R C D F C D
PRESSCUTTING
A L H R H O S C
COLLIERY SWITCH
I T P E M H A A
OXON INCIDENTAL
U D C N R U E
SOON RETIREMENT

11

SPITEFUL ALCOVE
O I U E N O I
SPRAWL TENEMENT
L R L F I E T
BARATHEA ENDEAR
R O L I G
DOUBLEDEALER
C E S E N S
CANDLESTICKS
N U H O G
ENACTS ONRECORD
I T P U A H A
OBLIGING TRAITS
A O N H E I I
GLANCE TIDINESS

12

COLOSSAL RANCID
A U A U T H R
DESOLATE GYRATE
G T A O P P A
EARDRUMS RIFLED
S E Y O I C A I
ABERRATION
F E R I R L N G
EASTERLIES
T T C E S A C S
CHILLY PORTRAIT
H M A L H R O
ITALIC FUNEREAL
N T M T N E I
GREASE MEASURED

Solutions 13-15

13

C		B		L				R		S		P		T
O	P	U	L	E	N	T		O	S	T	R	I	C	H
S		L		A		R		G		A		Q		E
M	E	L	O	D	R	A	M	A		B	L	U	R	B
O		S		I		P		N				E		L
S	T	E	I	N				J	U	J	I	T	S	U
		Y		G		P		O		O				E
M	E	E	T	M	E	I	N	S	T	L	O	U	I	S
E				A		N		H		L		N		
A	N	D	A	N	T	E				Y	A	C	H	T
T		Y				A		B		R		L		R
L	O	N	E	R		P	H	E	N	O	M	E	N	A
O		A		A		P		T		G		S		L
A	D	M	I	R	A	L		A	V	E	R	A	G	E
F		O		E		E				R		M		E

14

K	I	N	G	F	I	S	H	E	R		O	P	E	N
I		Y		O		H		N		H		L		E
B	A	L	E	R		R	A	T	I	O	N	A	L	E
O		O		T		I		E		T		C		D
S	U	N	B	U	R	N		R	A	W	D	E	A	L
H		S		N		K				A		B		E
			M	E	N	A	G	E	A	T	R	O	I	S
A		C		T		G		N		E		S		S
C	A	U	S	E	C	E	L	E	B	R	E			
C		T		L				R		B		U		S
R	E	G	U	L	A	R		G	R	O	W	N	U	P
E		L		E		A		I		T		W		I
D	I	A	T	R	I	B	E	S		T	R	I	E	D
I		S		S		B		E		L		N		E
T	A	S	K		M	I	N	D	R	E	A	D	E	R

15

P	A	N	A	M	A		G	A	S	M	E	T	E	R
	M		C		X		O		E		I		N	
B	E	S	T	S	E	L	L	E	R		D	O	D	O
	N		I		M		D		E		E		E	
E	D	E	N	T	A	T	E		N	O	R	M	A	L
			I		N		N		I				V	
W	O	O	D				R	O	T	A	T	I	O	N
	P		E		L		E		Y		E		U	
R	E	D	S	T	A	R	T				L	O	R	D
	R				B		R		S		E			
B	A	N	G	E	R		I	N	C	A	M	E	R	A
	T		R		A		E		A		E		O	
H	I	D	E		D	E	V	O	L	U	T	I	O	N
	V		E		O		E		E		E		S	
T	E	N	D	E	R	E	R		S	T	R	U	T	S

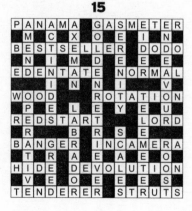

Solutions 16-18

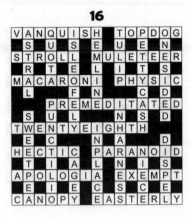

16

V	A	N	Q	U	I	S	H		T	O	P	D	O	G
	S		U		S		E		U		E		N	
S	T	R	O	L	L		M	U	L	E	T	E	E	R
	R		T		E		L		I		T		S	
M	A	C	A	R	O	N	I		P	H	Y	S	I	C
	L				F		N				C		D	
			P	R	E	M	E	D	I	T	A	T	E	D
	S		U		L				N		S		D	
T	W	E	N	T	Y	E	I	G	H	T	H			
	E		C				N		A				D	
H	E	C	T	I	C		P	A	R	A	N	O	I	D
	T		I		A		L		N		I		S	
A	P	O	L	O	G	I	A		E	X	E	M	P	T
	E		I		E		C		S		C		E	
C	A	N	O	P	Y		E	A	S	T	E	R	L	Y

17

B	A	L	L	A	D		A	C	H	I	L	L	E	S
R		I		D				O		N		A		E
A	B	L	A	Z	E		O	V	E	R	A	W	E	D
N		L		E		M		E		E		Y		A
D	R	I	P		C	A	I	R	O		B	E	S	T
I		P		A		I		C		O		R		E
S	T	U	F	F	E	D	S	H	I	R	T			
H		T		F		E		A		G		S		S
			D	I	N	N	E	R	J	A	C	K	E	T
A		H		X		S		G		N		E		A
S	H	E	D		S	P	I	E	L		P	L	A	Y
Y		R		T		E		S		G		E		A
L	I	O	N	S	D	E	N		K	O	W	T	O	W
U		I		A		C				S		O		A
M	O	N	A	R	C	H	Y		S	H	A	N	T	Y

18

M	I	S	S	I	S	S	I	P	P	I				A
A		L		M		A		R		N		G		N
C	H	A	M	P	A	G	N	E		A	L	O	N	G
H		S		U		E		T		N		S		E
I	N	H	A	L	E		R	E	V	E	R	S	A	L
N				S				N				A		I
E	A	R	W	I	G		A	C	A	D	E	M	I	C
		O		O		C		E		O		E		
B	R	A	I	N	B	O	X		A	M	O	R	E	T
A		D				S				I				R
T	I	R	E	S	O	M	E		E	N	C	O	R	E
T		A		P		E		G		I		K		S
E	A	G	L	E		T	R	E	N	C	H	A	N	T
R		E		E		I		A		A		P		L
Y				D	O	C	T	R	I	N	A	I	R	E

Solutions 19-21

19

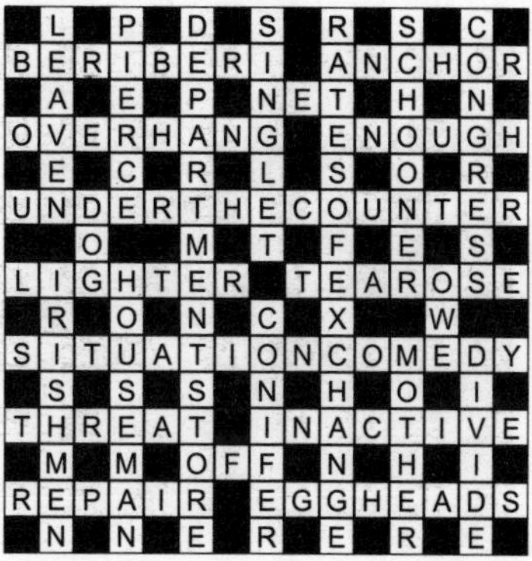

20

21

Solutions 22-24

22

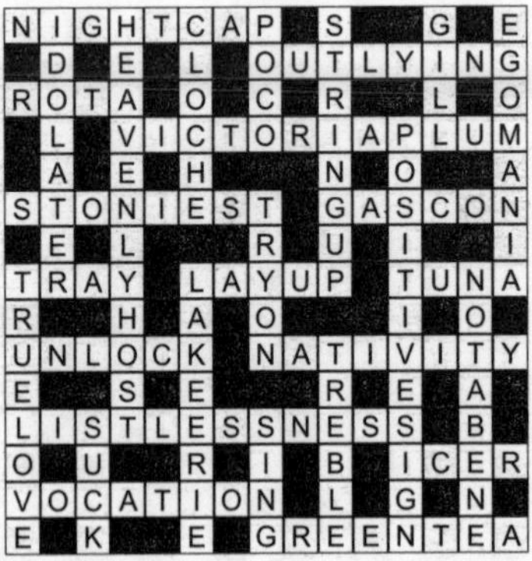

23

24

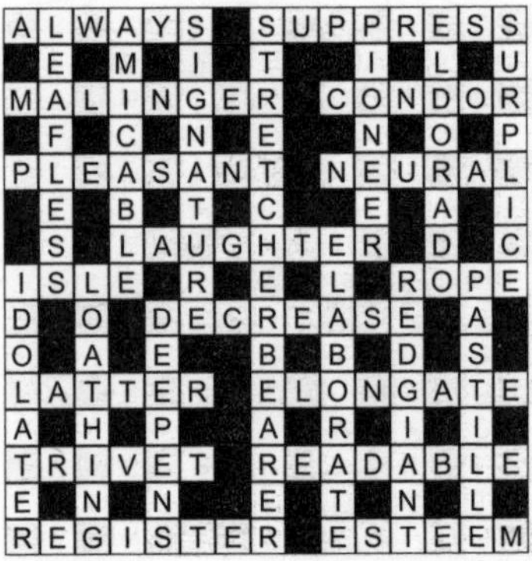

Solutions 25-27

25

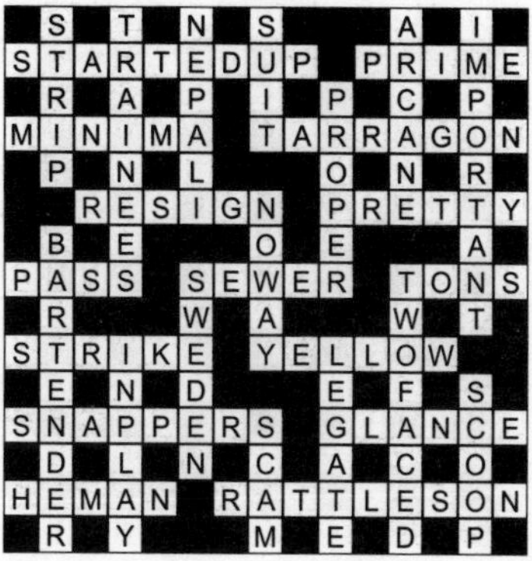

26

27

Solutions 28-30

28

S	T	U	C	C	O		F	O	O	T	S	T	E	P
O		N		A		P		N		A		O		A
M	A	S	O	N		A	B	E	R	N	E	T	H	Y
E		H		A		R		O		G		E		I
T	R	A	N	S	I	T		F	R	E	E	M	A	N
I		C		T		T		T		L				G
M	A	K	E	A	N	I	G	H	T	O	F	I	T	
E		L				M		O				N		D
	R	E	C	K	L	E	S	S	D	R	I	V	E	R
B				N		W		E		E		E		U
L	U	M	B	A	G	O		D	E	C	O	R	U	M
A		U		V		R		A		Y		S		B
M	A	S	T	E	R	K	E	Y		C	H	I	L	E
E		I		R		E		S		L		O		A
D	O	C	K	Y	A	R	D		P	E	A	N	U	T

29

S	I	T	R	E	P		T	E	N	T	A	C	L	E
	B		E		L		H		A		B		A	
W	I	N	G	M	I	R	R	O	R		B	U	C	K
	Z		R		G		O		C		O		O	
G	A	M	E	S	H	O	W		O	U	T	I	N	G
			T		T		I		T				I	
C	H	E	F				N	U	I	S	A	N	C	E
	O		U		S		O		C		N		A	
B	U	L	L	E	T	I	N				A	L	L	Y
	R				R		E		R		R			
A	G	E	N	D	A		S	E	A	S	C	A	P	E
	L		U		I		H		N		H		E	
P	A	I	R		G	R	A	N	D	P	I	A	N	O
	S		S		H		N		O		S		A	
A	S	S	E	N	T	E	D		M	E	T	T	L	E

30

	Q		I		S		S				C		C	
L	U	B	R	I	C	A	T	E		H	O	A	R	D
	I		R		R		A		D		O		I	
D	E	R	I	D	E		G	R	A	Y	L	I	N	G
	T		G		E				M		E		O	
		B	A	N	N	E	D		P	A	R	T	L	Y
	M		T				R		E				I	
R	I	T	E		A	D	O	R	N		D	A	N	E
	S				F		O				I		E	
B	E	L	I	E	F		P	O	P	L	A	R		
	R		N		A				L		B		C	
P	A	S	T	R	I	E	S		I	C	E	C	A	P
	B		O		R		A		A		T		D	
B	L	A	N	K		O	R	A	N	G	E	A	D	E
	E		E				I		T		S		Y	

Solutions 31-33

31

M	O	N	I	T	O	R	I	N	G		U	T	A	H
A		O		E		U		I				A		E
T	O	T	A	L		M	A	C	E	D	O	N	I	A
T		I		L		M		H		A		G		D
		C	O	M	R	A	D	E	I	N	A	R	M	S
P		E		E		G				C		A		T
R	E	D	F	A	C	E	D		D	I	M	M	E	R
O				N		D		P		N				O
P	O	M	P	O	M		D	R	A	G	O	M	A	N
A		O		T				E		M		A		G
G	E	T	T	H	E	M	E	S	S	A	G	E		
A		I		E		A		I		S		S		M
N	E	V	E	R	M	I	N	D		T	I	T	H	E
D		E				Z		E		E		R		A
A	L	S	O		T	E	N	D	E	R	L	O	I	N

32

		I	N	C	A	N	D	E	S	C	E	N	T	
J		M		L		O		A		O		O		M
U	M	P	T	E	E	N		S	A	T	S	U	M	A
S		A		A		E		E		E		R		R
T	E	L	A	V	I	V		D	E	R	R	I	C	K
I		E		E		E				I		S		E
F	A	D	E	S		N	I	S	S	E	N	H	U	T
I						T		E						G
C	H	A	S	T	I	S	E	D		P	A	S	T	A
A		V		U				U		R		E		R
T	R	O	P	I	C	S		C	R	E	A	S	E	D
I		C		T		O		T		C		S		E
O	R	A	T	I	O	N		I	B	E	R	I	A	N
N		D		O		I		O		D		O		S
	G	O	I	N	G	C	O	N	C	E	R	N		

33

B	I	R	D	C	A	G	E		S	C	O	R	C	H
I		E		L		O				U		A		E
C	A	C	H	A	L	O	T		C	R	U	M	B	S
A		I		R		D		S		T		B		I
R	I	T	U	A	L	I	S	M		A	D	U	L	T
B		E				S		O		I		T		A
			R	I	C	H		G	A	L	L	A	N	T
E		P		N						E		N		E
P	L	U	M	A	G	E		M	A	D	E			
I		B		M		A		A				D		S
D	E	L	H	I		S	A	C	R	A	M	E	N	T
E		I		N		T		E		L		C		O
M	O	C	K	U	P		A	D	D	I	T	I	O	N
I		A		T				O		S		D		E
C	A	N	T	E	R		E	N	D	T	O	E	N	D

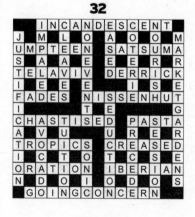

Solutions 34-36

34

35

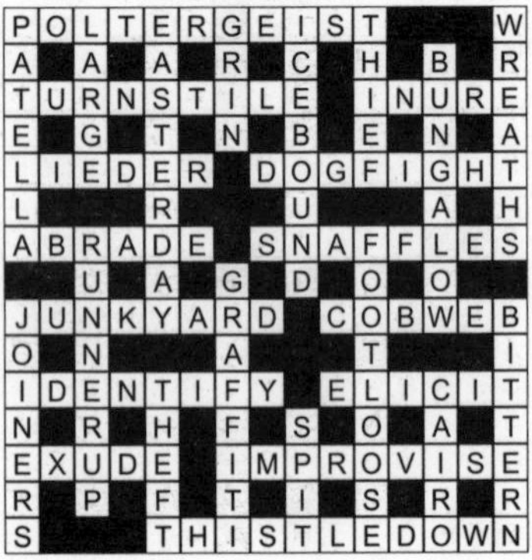

36

Solutions 37-39

37

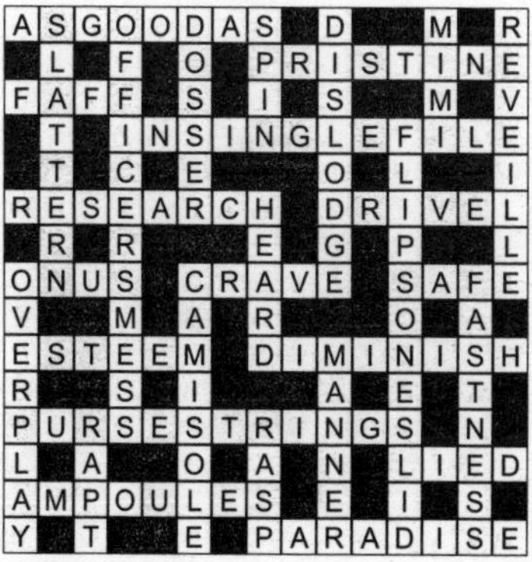

38

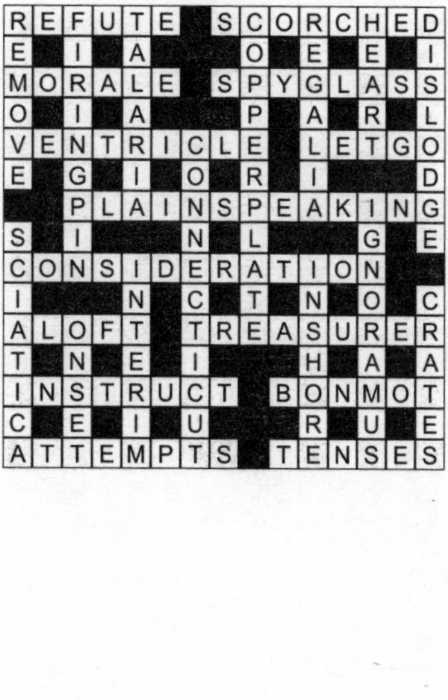

39

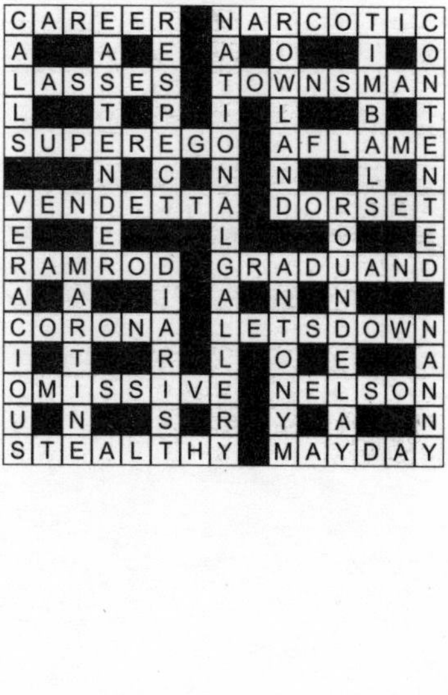

Solutions 40-42

40

41

42

Solutions 43-45

43

■	■	S	E	C	R	E	T	A	R	I	E	S	■	■
■	■	P	■	H	■	N	■	R	■	M	■	P	■	■
S	A	I	L	I	N	G	■	R	E	P	L	I	E	D
T	■	N	■	M	■	A	■	E	■	A	■	N	■	A
A	G	A	P	E	■	R	E	S	E	R	V	O	I	R
Y	■	C	■	■	■	D	■	T	■	T	■	S	■	E
A	C	H	I	E	V	E	■	S	H	I	N	E	R	S
T	■	■	■	L	■	■	■	■	■	A	■	■	■	S
H	O	S	T	A	G	E	■	F	E	L	U	C	C	A
O	■	A	■	B	■	M	■	L	■	■	■	O	■	L
M	E	L	I	O	R	A	T	E	■	S	E	N	N	A
E	■	L	■	R	■	N	■	A	■	T	■	C	■	A
S	P	I	R	A	E	A	■	P	E	R	F	O	R	M
■	■	E	■	T	■	T	■	I	■	I	■	R	■	■
■	■	S	T	E	R	E	O	T	Y	P	E	D	■	■

44

S	T	A	N	D	I	N	G	■	T	R	O	P	I	C
T	■	G	■	E	■	■	O	■	■	E	■	O	■	A
R	E	A	L	M	■	P	O	L	Y	E	S	T	E	R
E	■	T	■	O	■	R	■	I	■	D	■	B	■	E
S	P	E	L	L	B	O	U	N	D	■	L	O	A	F
S	■	■	■	I	■	T	■	E	■	R	■	I	■	R
■	■	K	I	S	S	A	N	D	T	E	L	L	■	E
S	K	I	■	H	■	G	■	R	■	A	■	E	V	E
C	■	T	E	E	T	O	T	A	L	L	E	R	■	■
R	■	C	■	D	■	N	■	W	■	M	■	■	■	L
A	C	H	E	■	M	I	L	I	T	A	R	I	S	E
M	■	E	■	N	■	S	■	N	■	D	■	D	■	S
B	U	N	D	E	S	T	A	G	■	R	A	I	D	S
L	■	E	■	W	■	■	S	■	■	I	■	O	■	O
E	R	R	A	T	A	■	H	A	N	D	Y	M	A	N

45

F	R	E	E	F	O	R	A	L	L	■	M	I	D	I
U	■	N	■	I	■	E	■	A	■	■	■	C	■	L
S	P	U	R	N	■	M	A	R	M	O	R	E	A	L
E	■	M	■	A	■	A	■	V	■	N	■	B	■	I
■	■	B	A	N	K	S	T	A	T	E	M	E	N	T
C	■	E	■	C	■	T	■	■	■	N	■	R	■	E
H	E	R	O	I	N	E	S	■	G	I	N	G	E	R
O	■	■	■	A	■	R	■	S	■	G	■	■	■	A
P	I	C	K	L	E	■	P	A	T	H	E	T	I	C
S	■	H	■	Y	■	■	■	B	■	T	■	E	■	Y
T	R	I	C	E	R	A	T	O	P	S	E	S	■	■
I	■	M	■	A	■	P	■	T	■	T	■	S	■	M
C	I	N	E	R	A	R	I	A	■	A	R	E	N	A
K	■	E	■	■	■	O	■	G	■	N	■	R	■	R
S	O	Y	A	■	I	N	C	E	N	D	I	A	R	Y

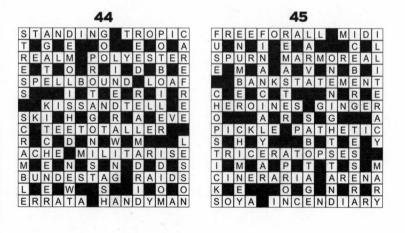

Solutions 46-48

46

SECONDWIND PACK
Q A A E O I A
UNSETTLE GALORE
A T U L H O D
DARKROOM OXTAIL
R O E I U I N
O LOSS N A
NOTABLE PERGOLA
N U ADZE M
T D S C C M E
SHRIFT JUBILANT
E E C L R R H
HERNIA SANCTITY
B C L T U O S
OBOE LOVERSKNOT

47

ADDICT PARADISE
P U E C T G R
TACKLE SCHOONER
I H L D O M O A
TIED CRAMP WREN
U S B E P S E D
DISCONSOLATE
E E G S I E I G
JULIUSCAESAR
S D S N H K T A
USER AGREE PAID
P M T D D T N I
EXECUTOR BAUBLE
R A B W X U N
BANDANNA BILLET

48

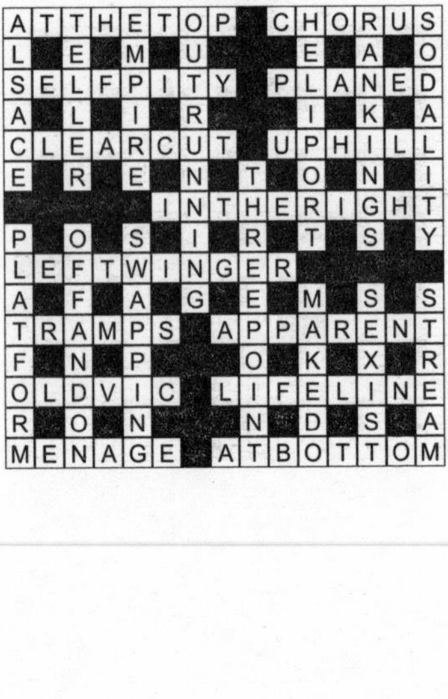
ATTHETOP CHORUS
L E M U E A O
SELFPITY PLANED
A L I R I K A
CLEARCUT UPHILL
E R E N T O N I
INTHERIGHT
P O S I R T S Y
LEFTWINGER
A F A G E M S S
TRAMPS APPARENT
F N P O K X R
OLDVIC LIFELINE
R O N N D S A
MENAGE ATBOTTOM

Solutions 49-51

49

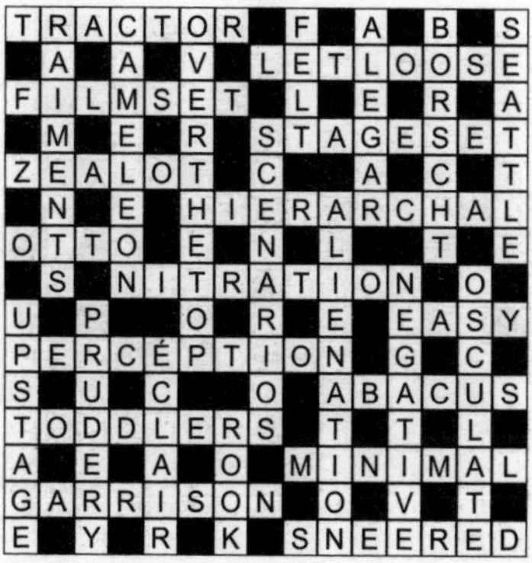

50

51

Solutions 52-54

52

53

54

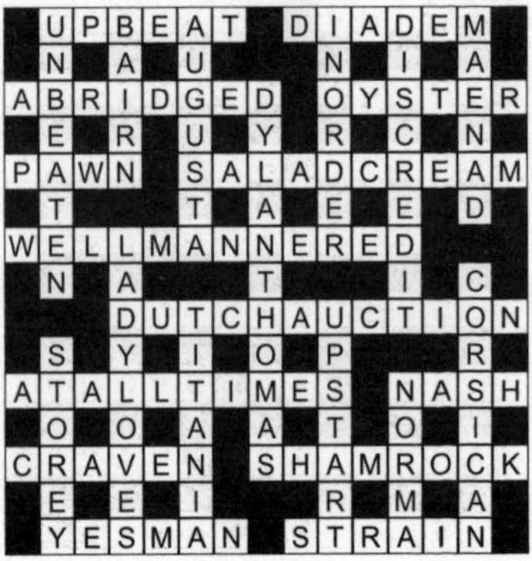

Solutions 55-57

55

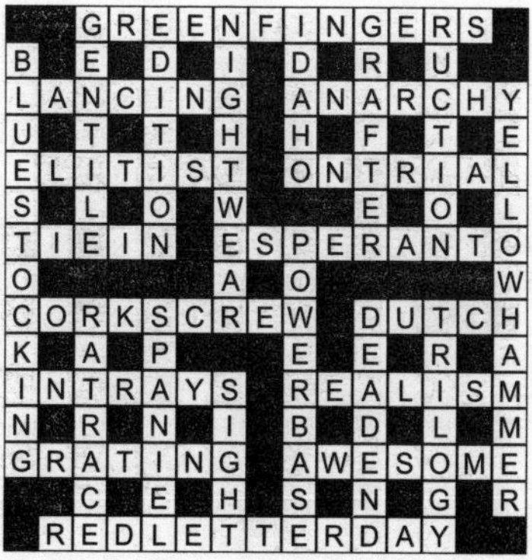

56

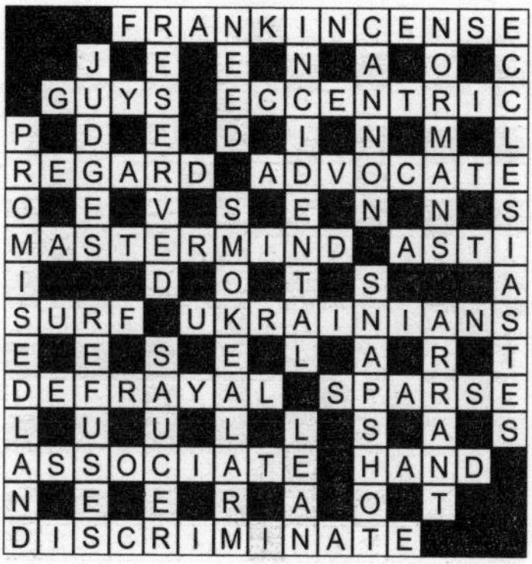

57

Solutions 58-60

58

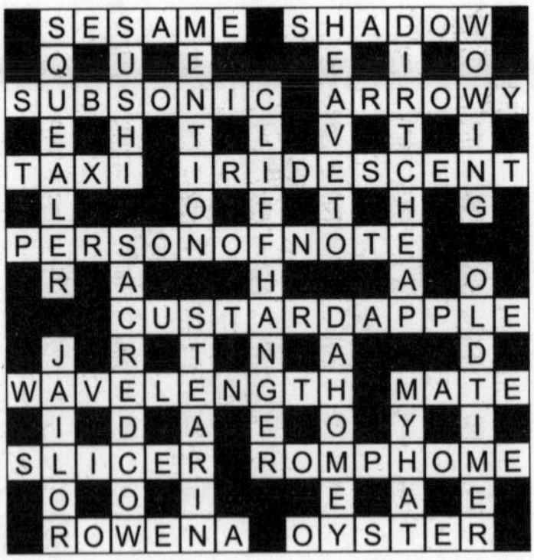

59

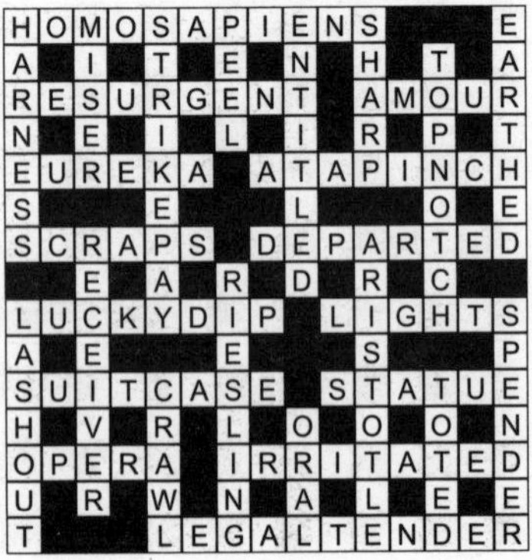

60

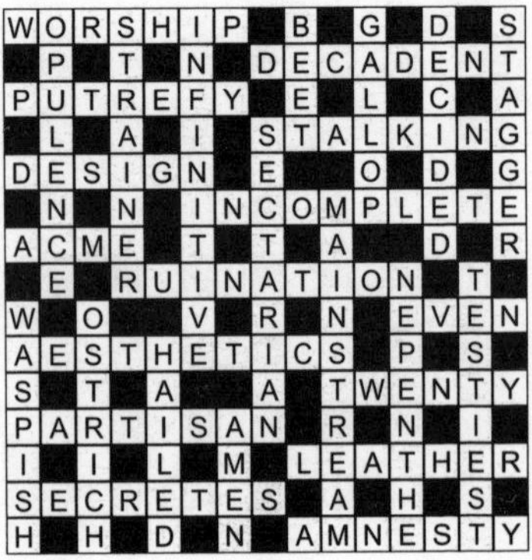

Solutions 61-63

61

62

63

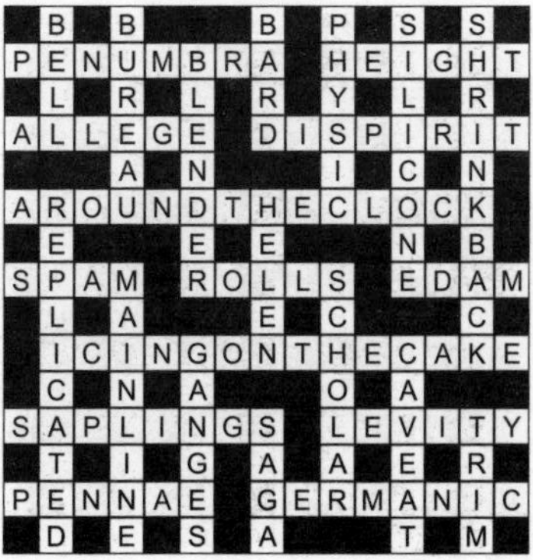

Solutions 64-66

64

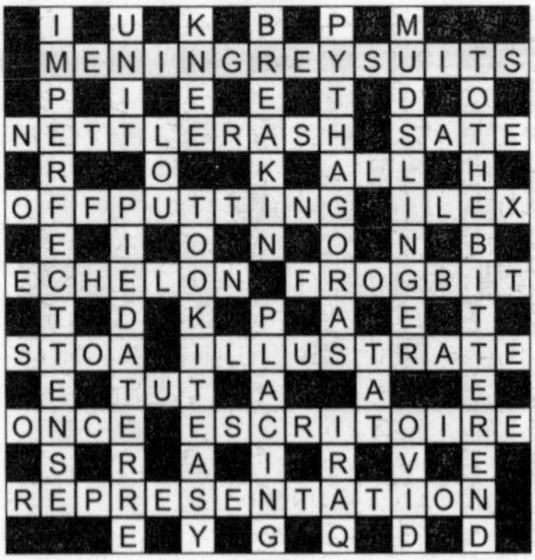

65

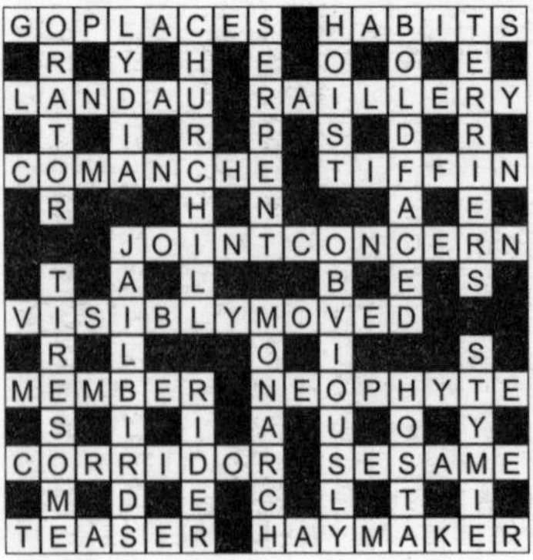

66

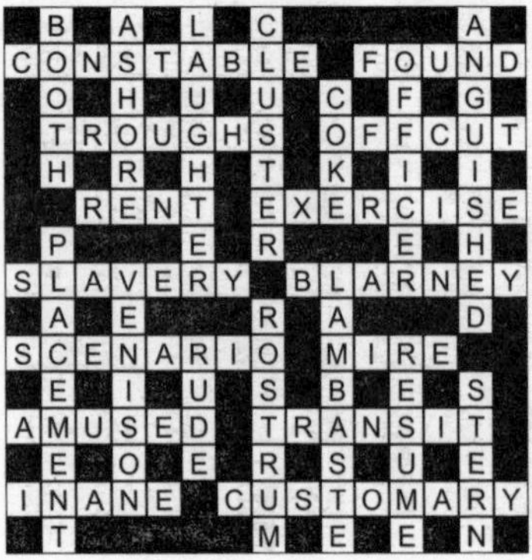

Solutions 67-69

67

	W		B		P				M		S		D	
F	A	I	R	F	A	X		F	E	A	T	H	E	R
	G		A		R		L		A		A		P	
P	O	S	S	E	S	S	I	O	N		T	O	O	T
	N				E		E		T		I		S	
W	E	L	L	R	E	A	D		I	R	O	N	I	C
	R		E				E		M		N		T	
		C	A	R	R	Y	T	H	E	C	A	N		
	F		D		E		E				R		I	
M	A	R	I	O	N		C	U	R	R	Y	I	N	G
	C		N		T		T		O				S	
S	T	A	G		F	O	O	T	L	I	G	H	T	S
	I		M		R		R		L		I		A	
D	O	W	A	G	E	R		B	U	F	F	A	L	O
	N		N		E				P		T		L	

68

S	T	I	T	C	H		N	E	E	D	L	E	S	S
	I		R		A		A		U		Y		A	
S	T	R	A	I	G	H	T	E	R		I	O	W	A
	H		F		G		I		O		N		H	
S	E	R	A	G	L	I	O		P	I	G	E	O	N
			L		E		N		E				R	
S	N	A	G				A	L	A	R	M	I	S	T
	U		A		S		L		N		O		E	
S	M	A	R	T	I	N	G				V	I	S	A
	B				G		A		S		I			
N	E	L	S	O	N		L	I	Q	U	E	U	R	S
	R		T		P		L		U		S		A	
E	T	N	A		O	V	E	R	A	C	T	I	V	E
	E		T		S		R		R		A		E	
A	N	C	E	S	T	R	Y		E	R	R	I	N	G

69

C	O	M	E	L	Y		S	T	O	P	O	V	E	R
U		A		A				A		A		O		U
T	A	K	I	N	G		S	K	E	L	E	T	O	N
O		E		T				E		M		E		A
F	I	S	H	E	R	M	A	N		T	H	R	O	W
F		H		R		A		I		O				A
		I	N	N	O	C	E	N	T	P	A	R	T	Y
H		F				H		H				A		S
A	U	T	H	O	R	I	T	A	R	I	A	N		
R				N		N		N		N		D		A
D	O	W	S	E		A	U	D	A	C	I	O	U	S
S		E		S		T				E		M		S
H	O	L	S	T	E	I	N		E	N	D	I	V	E
I		L		E		O				S		S		R
P	O	S	T	P	O	N	E		D	E	C	E	N	T

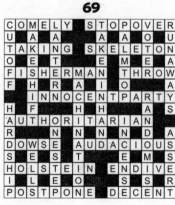

Solutions 70-72

70

C	■	B	■	I	N	C	A	S	E	■	C	U	B	E
A	B	R	I	M	■	A	■	P	■	■	A	■	A	■
L	■	I	■	P	O	N	Y	E	X	P	R	E	S	S
F	U	D	G	E	■	D	■	C	■	■	O	■	I	■
■	■	G	■	D	R	I	V	I	N	G	B	A	C	K
E	■	E	■	I	■	D	■	M	■	O	■	L	■	I
M	A	D	A	M	E	■	H	E	S	I	T	A	N	T
B	■	R	■	E	■	H	■	N	■	N	■	R	■	S
R	H	I	A	N	N	O	N	■	A	G	A	M	I	C
Y	■	V	■	T	■	N	■	P	■	S	■	S	■	H
O	P	E	N	A	N	D	S	H	U	T	■	Y	■	■
■	E	■	E	■	■	U	■	E	■	R	I	S	E	R
A	C	C	E	L	E	R	A	N	D	O	■	T	■	U
■	A	■	D	■	■	A	■	O	■	N	O	E	N	D
E	N	V	Y	■	U	N	P	L	U	G	■	M	■	D

71

P	O	U	N	D	S	■	O	B	S	T	A	C	L	E
A	■	P	■	A	■	■	■	E	■	I	■	H	■	G
S	I	S	K	I	N	■	W	A	G	E	R	I	N	G
T	■	T	■	S	■	P	■	T	■	S	■	L	■	S
I	V	A	N	■	T	R	I	T	E	■	E	L	M	O
C	■	I	■	S	■	E	■	H	■	I	■	I	■	N
H	A	R	D	T	O	P	L	E	A	S	E	■	■	■
E	■	S	■	O	■	O	■	C	■	S	■	P	■	U
■	■	■	H	O	R	S	D	O	E	U	V	R	E	S
C	■	A	■	P	■	T	■	U	■	E	■	A	■	E
H	I	V	E	■	M	E	A	N	S	■	A	C	I	D
O	■	E	■	B	■	R	■	T	■	B	■	T	■	T
P	E	N	T	A	G	O	N	■	C	A	S	I	N	O
I	■	U	■	W	■	U	■	■	■	S	■	C	■	I
N	E	E	D	L	E	S	S	■	D	E	T	E	S	T

72

S	H	A	N	G	H	A	I	■	C	O	R	S	E	T
O	■	D	■	E	■	N	■	■	■	P	■	A	■	E
L	E	M	O	N	A	D	E	■	M	A	R	L	I	N
A	■	I	■	E	■	Y	■	A	■	Q	■	V	■	D
C	U	R	A	R	E	■	O	B	D	U	R	A	T	E
E	■	E	■	O	■	O	■	A	■	E	■	G	■	R
■	■	■	H	U	S	B	A	N	D	■	M	E	T	E
N	■	B	■	S	■	S	■	D	■	A	■	D	■	R
A	C	I	D	■	A	C	C	O	S	T	S	■	■	■
U	■	G	■	E	■	E	■	N	■	R	■	A	■	C
T	R	A	I	N	I	N	G	■	P	O	N	C	H	O
I	■	M	■	T	■	E	■	F	■	P	■	A	■	H
C	H	O	P	I	N	■	M	E	D	I	O	C	R	E
A	■	U	■	R	■	■	■	T	■	N	■	I	■	R
L	E	S	S	E	N	■	D	E	L	E	G	A	T	E

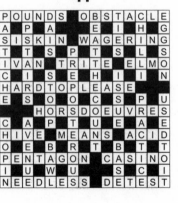

Solutions 73-75

73

	F		A		S		H				W		U	
R	E	D	S	E	T	T	E	R		D	I	A	N	E
	V		T		R		A		B		S		S	
J	E	R	E	M	I	A	D		A	N	T	H	E	M
	R		R		K		S		L		E		T	
		A	N	T	I		E	M	I	G	R	A	T	E
	D				N		T				I		L	
S	A	U	S	A	G	E		P	A	L	A	V	E	R
	S		U				O		T				D	
C	H	A	P	L	A	I	N		T	I	C	K		
	B		P		W		A		O		A		C	
C	O	O	L	E	R		D	A	R	I	N	G	L	Y
	A		A		Y		I		N		A		O	
G	R	A	N	D		C	E	L	E	B	R	I	T	Y
	D		T				T		Y		D		H	

74

T	R	A	V	E	R	S	E	D		E	X	A	C	T
A		R		N		I		I		N		R		H
N	E	E	D	L	E	S		S		A		I		R
D		C		I		T	O	T	E	M	P	O	L	E
O		A		S		E		A		O		S		S
O	R	N	A	T	E	R		N	O	R	W	I	C	H
R		U						C		E				
I	N	T	E	R	D	E	P	E	N	D	E	N	C	E
				A		Y						E		N
S	E	A	T	T	L	E		C	O	N	T	E	N	T
C		C		I		S		O		A		D		R
O	R	A	T	O	R	I	O	S		T		L		U
U		C		N		G		S	E	T	T	E	R	S
T		I		A		H		I		E		S		T
S	T	A	L	L		T	H	E	O	R	I	S	E	S

75

F		B		A		S		R		L		D		L
L	E	A	R	N		T	H	E	M	E	T	U	N	E
E		S		N		A		D		F		C		A
D	R	A	G	O	U	T		D	I	T	C	H	E	D
		L		D		E		W				E		I
S	E	T	T	O		D	E	A	D	L	Y	S	I	N
O				M				R		O		S		G
L	E	T	T	I	N	G	O	F	F	S	T	E	A	M
I		A		N		U				T				A
D	E	C	L	I	N	I	N	G		C	A	B	I	N
A		K				D		A		A		U		
R	E	L	A	P	S	E		L	A	U	N	D	E	R
I		I		O		D		E		S		G		I
T	O	N	E	S	D	O	W	N		E	M	E	N	D
Y		G		E		G		A		S		T		E

Solutions 76-78

76

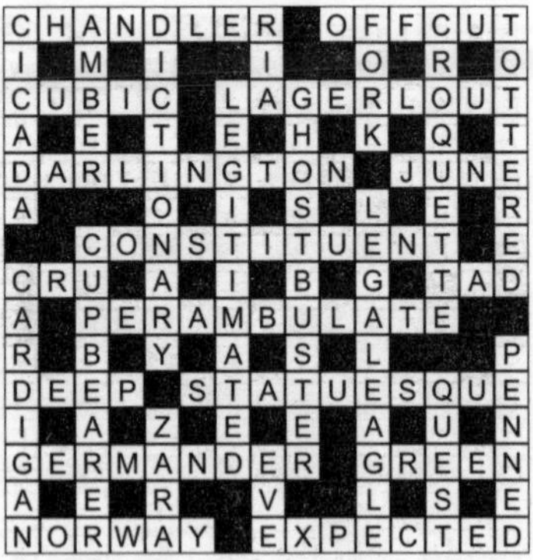

77

78

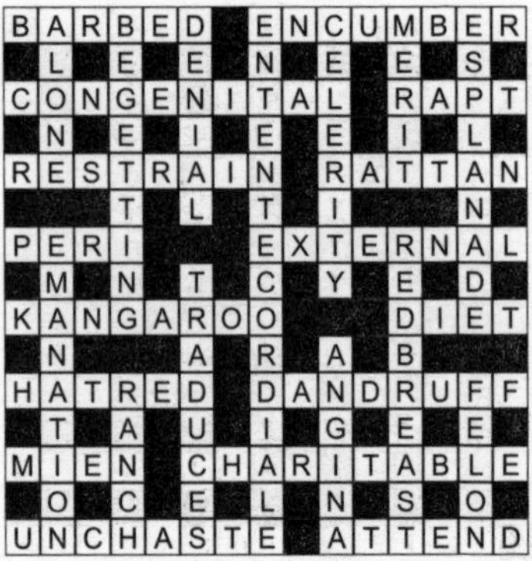

Solutions 79-81

79

P	A	S	T	O	R	■	■	■	F	I	A	S	C	O
A	■	A	■	V	■	B	A	R	■	V	■	K	■	R
R	A	W	D	E	A	L	■	E	L	Y	S	I	A	N
A	■	M	■	R	■	O	■	S	■	L	■	D	■	A
D	R	I	F	T	■	O	N	T	H	E	T	R	O	T
E	■	L	■	■	■	D	■	A	■	A	■	O	■	E
■	A	L	I	C	E	B	L	U	E	G	O	W	N	■
■	R	■	■	H	■	R	■	R	■	U	■	■	Y	■
■	M	A	D	I	S	O	N	A	V	E	N	U	E	■
S	■	W	■	N	■	T	■	N	■	■	■	P	■	S
L	I	K	E	A	S	H	O	T	■	S	T	R	U	T
O	■	W	■	T	■	E	■	C	■	P	■	I	■	R
G	L	A	M	O	U	R	■	A	L	L	E	G	R	O
A	■	R	■	W	■	S	I	R	■	I	■	H	■	K
N	A	D	I	N	E	■	■	■	S	T	A	T	U	E

80

S	H	O	U	L	D	E	R	B	L	A	D	E	S	■
■	■	C	■	A	■	Q	■	L	■	D	■	M	■	P
■	M	A	N	I	C	U	R	E	■	M	O	U	S	E
P	■	R	■	R	■	I	■	A	■	I	■	L	■	R
R	A	I	D	■	S	P	O	R	T	S	C	A	R	S
I	■	N	■	R	■	P	■	Y	■	S	■	T	■	I
C	H	A	R	A	D	E	S	■	W	I	D	E	N	S
K	■	■	■	C	■	D	■	C	■	O	■	■	■	T
L	A	C	K	E	Y	■	M	A	I	N	L	I	N	E
Y	■	R	■	C	■	U	■	T	■	S	■	M	■	N
P	R	O	P	O	U	N	D	E	D	■	E	P	I	C
E	■	U	■	U	■	W	■	R	■	W	■	E	■	E
A	C	T	O	R	■	E	M	I	G	R	A	T	E	■
R	■	O	■	S	■	L	■	N	■	E	■	U	■	■
■	I	N	T	E	L	L	I	G	E	N	T	S	I	A

81

R	E	P	A	S	T	■	■	■	H	O	U	S	E	S
E	■	A	■	P	■	F	U	R	■	V	■	T	■	T
C	O	R	S	I	C	A	■	O	N	E	T	I	M	E
I	■	T	■	K	■	I	■	G	■	R	■	P	■	R
P	L	I	N	Y	■	R	O	U	G	H	H	E	W	N
E	■	T	■	■	■	A	■	E	■	E	■	N	■	A
■	C	A	Y	M	A	N	I	S	L	A	N	D	S	■
■	O	■	■	A	■	D	■	G	■	R	■	■	A	■
■	G	R	A	N	D	S	T	A	N	D	I	N	G	■
S	■	A	■	N	■	Q	■	L	■	■	■	E	■	L
P	E	R	P	E	T	U	A	L	■	P	I	T	T	A
A	■	E	■	R	■	A	■	E	■	A	■	W	■	W
T	U	B	B	I	E	R	■	R	E	C	T	O	R	Y
H	■	I	■	S	■	E	L	Y	■	E	■	R	■	E
E	N	T	O	M	B	■	■	■	B	R	O	K	E	R

The Telegraph

Solutions 82-84

82

83

84

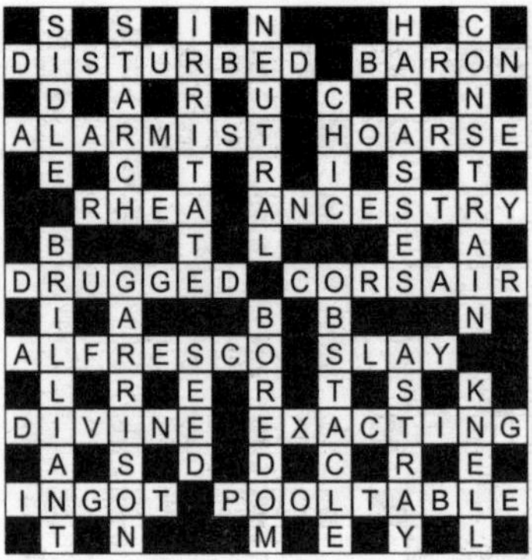

Solutions 85-87

85

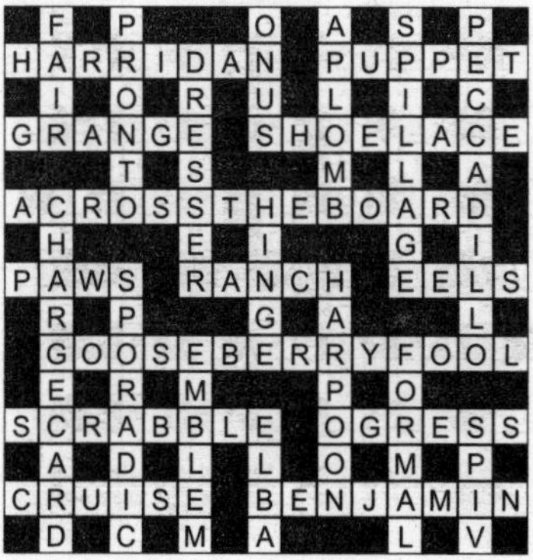

86

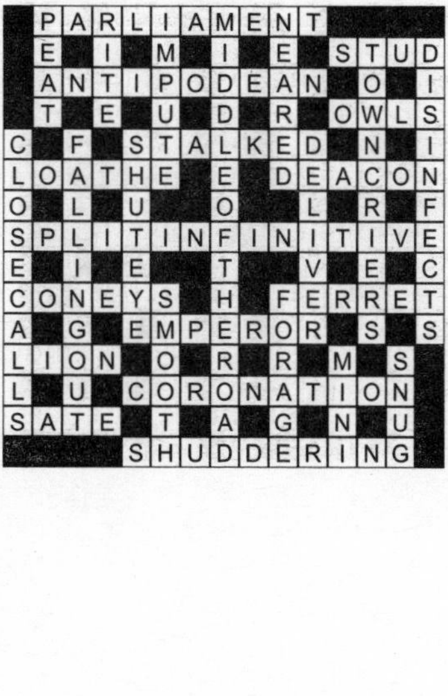

87

Solutions 88-90

88

89

90

Solutions 91-93

91

G		B		M		S		G		D		D		U
A	N	I	T	A		T	R	A	G	E	D	I	A	N
G		S		D		A		R		A		S		A
A	T	H	E	A	R	T		R	I	N	G	L	E	T
		O		G		I		I				O		T
A	L	P	H	A		C	A	S	S	A	N	D	R	A
S				S				O		P		G		C
T	H	E	I	C	E	M	A	N	C	O	M	E	T	H
R		N		A		A				S				E
O	R	D	E	R	A	R	M	S		T	E	P	I	D
L		A				K		E		R		O		
O	M	N	I	B	U	S		C	H	O	P	P	E	R
G		G		A		M		O		P		O		I
E	V	E	R	G	R	E	E	N		H	A	U	N	T
R		R		S		N		D		E		T		Z

92

P	A	R	E	N	T	H	E	S	I	S				C
I		U		O		O		P		A		L		A
B	A	L	T	I	M	O	R	E		D	E	A	L	T
R		E		S		P		L		H		U		E
O	R	D	A	I	N		F	L	O	U	N	D	E	R
C				N				I				A		E
H	A	I	L	E	D		S	N	A	C	K	B	A	R
		N		S		W		G		H		L		
R	E	V	I	S	I	O	N		P	O	T	E	N	T
U		I				R				R				R
S	E	T	B	A	C	K	S		F	I	A	S	C	O
T		I		L		S		H		S		A		U
L	E	N	T	O		H	E	A	R	T	B	U	R	N
E		G		H		O		L		E		N		C
S				A	P	P	R	O	P	R	I	A	T	E

93

			C	A	T	E	R	P	I	L	L	A	R	S
		D		N		M		O		I		U		T
	D	O	W	N		M	E	S	S	E	N	G	E	R
C		S		E		A		T		D		U		A
U	S	A	B	L	E		S	O	M	E	R	S	E	T
P		G		I		I		F		R		T		O
B	R	E	A	D	K	N	I	F	E		L	A	O	S
O				S		C		I		E				P
A	L	A	S		H	O	T	C	H	P	O	T	C	H
R		U		F		H		E		H		I		E
D	O	G	T	I	R	E	D		L	E	T	T	E	R
L		M		E		R		S		M		B		E
O	V	E	R	S	L	E	E	P		E	M	I	R	
V		N		T		N		A		R		T		
E	X	T	R	A	C	T	O	R	F	A	N			

Solutions 94-96

94

Q	U	I	C	K	T	E	M	P	E	R		I		W
	N		H		A			O		H	I	N	G	E
A	T	T	A	I	N	D	E	R		O		C		N
	I		M		Z			T	E	D	I	O	U	S
J	E	T	B	L	A	C	K			E		G		L
O			E		N		N	U	I	S	A	N	C	E
K	N	A	R		I		E			I		I		Y
I		F		V	A	N	E	S	S	A		T		D
N		T		E			C		H		S	O	Y	A
G	R	E	E	N	T	E	A		A		P			L
A		R		E			P	E	N	Z	A	N	C	E
P	A	N	C	R	A	S			G		T		R	
A		O		A		H	U	S	H	M	O	N	E	Y
R	O	O	S	T		O			A		W		W	
T		N		E	X	P	E	R	I	E	N	C	E	D

95

A	P	P	E	A	L		W	R	I	T	E	O	F	F
C		U		C				O		A		R		A
C	A	B	E	R	S		E	Y	E	S	I	G	H	T
U		C		E		O		A		K		A		H
R	A	R	E		S	L	I	L	Y		K	N	E	E
A		A		P		D		M		M		S		R
T	O	W	E	R	O	F	B	A	B	E	L			
E		L		O		A		R		A		C		S
			Q	U	E	S	T	I	O	N	M	A	R	K
H		S		D		H		N		S		M		Y
E	S	P	Y		T	I	L	E	R		O	P	A	L
A		R		S		O		S		R		A		I
D	R	I	P	P	I	N	G		L	A	C	I	N	G
E		N		A		E				S		G		H
R	A	G	T	R	A	D	E		W	H	Y	N	O	T

96

	F		M		P				D		T		S	
M	O	R	I	B	U	N	D		I	S	R	A	E	L
	R		S		R		E		D		A		A	
M	E	S	S		S	U	S	T	A	I	N	I	N	G
	C				U		E		C		S		C	
H	A	S	S	L	E		R	E	T	A	I	L	E	D
	S		T				T		I		T			
	T	R	E	M	O	R		A	C	R	O	S	S	
			N		B		A				R		I	
S	T	A	T	U	T	E	S		D	R	Y	A	D	S
	A		O		A		L		O				E	
E	X	O	R	B	I	T	A	N	T		T	A	R	N
	I		I		N		N		A		W		E	
I	N	N	A	T	E		T	E	R	M	I	N	A	L
	G		N		D				D		G		L	

Solutions 97-99

97

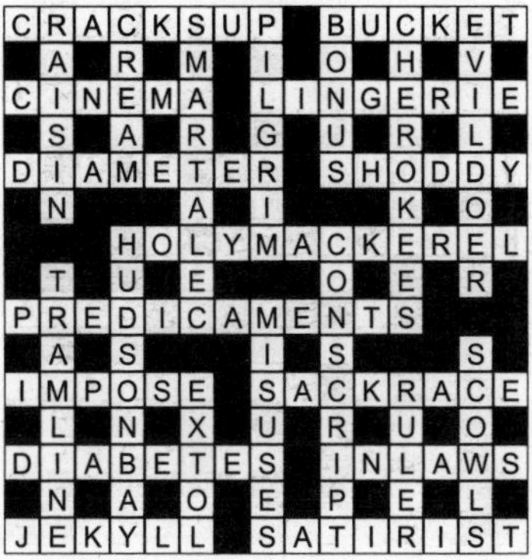

98

99

The Telegraph

01780

417271

Solution 100

100

		C	O	M	E	I	N	S	E	C	O	N	D	
S		H		I		N		E		L		A		
T	R	A	I	L		C	A	R	D	A	M	O	N	S
A		S		E		U		O		S		M		C
I	N	T	E	R	P	R	E	T		S	M	I	T	H
N		E						O		M				O
E	I	N	D	H	O	V	E	N		A	W	E	T	O
D		E		A		A		I		T		X		L
G	I	D	D	Y		M	A	N	N	E	R	I	S	M
L				S		P						S		A
A	L	E	R	T		I	N	D	I	C	A	T	E	S
S		V		A		R		I		O		E		T
S	T	A	N	C	H	I	O	N		R	A	N	G	E
		D		K		S		E		G		C		R
	N	E	W	S	H	E	A	D	L	I	N	E		

6VQ2B